16.3

OA 4737 16/10/77

*The Management of
Curriculum Development*

The Management of Curriculum Development

J. G. OWEN

CAMBRIDGE
At the University Press 1973

Published by the Syndics of the Cambridge University Press
Bentley House, 200 Euston Road, London NW1 2DB
American Branch: 32 East 57th Street, New York NY10022

© Cambridge University Press 1973

Library of Congress Catalogue Card Number: 72-97876

ISBNs:
0 521 20195 0 hard covers
0 521 09806 8 paperback

First published 1973

Printed in Great Britain
by C. Tinling & Co. Ltd
London and Prescot

Contents

PART ONE

What is curriculum made of?   3

1 *Growth of the idea of curriculum*   5
   Origins of change   5
   Restrictions   10

2 *Who should be in charge of curriculum?*   14
   Where does responsibility lie?   17
   New and traditional responsibilities   20
   Summary   22

3 *Examinations and the curriculum*   25
   Dissatisfaction with examinations   26
   Attempts to ease the worst effects of examinations   28
   Are examinations and curriculum inseparable?   30
   A new view of assessment   34
   Summary   36

4 *Other forces in the curriculum*   37
   Do different pressures create different curricula?   38
   Publications: the textbook   39
   Publications: the official voice   42
   Givers of advice   44
   Summary   48

PART TWO

Truisms   53

5 *Current English systems of curriculum development: the national picture*   57
   National plan and process   59
   No guidelines   64
   What do teachers need?   66
   Differences of response to national change   67

	Local diffusion and reform	69
	Who has any power of management?	70
	Responsibility in teachers' centres	72
	Summary	77
6	*The obstruction of development*	79
	Justifying improvement	79
	The uncertainty of a head teacher	80
	Frameworks for improvement: the school	81
	Out-of-school	83
	National ideals and local resistance	85
	Confusions and misuse	89
	Sales resistance	92
	Summary	93
7	*Local development: schools and teachers' centres*	95
	A primary school	97
	The dissatisfaction of assistant teachers	98
	How do teachers organise themselves?	99
	Interest, stimulus and teachers' centres	100
	Inspectors, advisers and the local management of change	102
	Summary	106
8	*Curriculum development and teacher education*	108
	Present forms of in-service training	110
	Continuous training: teachers' associations	112
	Continuous training: local education authorities	113
	Forms of training	114
	Training for management	116
	Training in the use of resources	120
	Models and micro-teaching	120
	The physical setting	124
	Individualisation of learning	126
	Summary	128
9	*Movements, plans and fashions*	132
	The movement towards family grouping	132
	Planned reform: team teaching	137
	Planned reform: integrated studies	140
	Planned reform: non-streaming	145
	Broader participation in reform	147
	De-schooling	153
	Summary	157

10	*Is there a future for curriculum development?*	159
	The teacher and the system	160
	The future of the system	161
	Choices about basic resources	164
	Summary	165
	Bibliography	167
	Index	175

PART ONE

What is curriculum made of?

The answer differs from generation to generation. In the same way as it has been claimed that the twentieth century has seen the first of our major preoccupations with productivity, with the acquisition of goods and with not only creating change but keeping up with change within the industrial field, so the same thing may be true of education.

The nineteenth century had been a period of great stability. Schools had changed very little between the nineteenth and the early twentieth century and although the word curriculum was in use it was very ill-defined; it seems usually to have amounted to very little more than a collection of syllabuses or a collection of subjects.

The first question that has to be settled by anyone who wants to start on the task of managing curriculum development is to find out what it is that he is managing. It may be that it is a mirage, that curriculum is too nebulous and that the development of it, therefore, is also something too slippery and altogether too indefinable to merit serious work. Despite this, the language of curriculum development is in use and the least that can be done when words are in vogue is to attempt to translate vogue into fashion and fashion into action.

The first section of this book will try to study how the idea of curriculum came about, how it changed, and how it came to acquire the meaning which it has today. Later we shall be able to look at the question of curriculum development as a significant subject in its totality. It may well after all be something which is *simply* a matter of fashion. It could be that this part of the twentieth century demands that those of us in education should pay attention to the content and method of learning, to the process and theory and philosophy of learning rather more closely than to the externalities of schooling, to buildings, to teachers, and to the jobs which our pupils will take when they leave school. For the time being the language of curriculum has a significance which it has not had for many years. Because of this it is important that we understand as much about it as we can.

1 Growth of the idea of curriculum

Ideas about curriculum have continuously and subtly altered for the past century and a half; the official view of what it should achieve has sometimes been voiced loudly, at other times more mutedly. There have been periods when it has seemed that curriculum was taken so much for granted that there was no need to re-examine it; but there have also been periods of considerable official interest.

It is important to understand the enthusiasms and apathies of the past; the present time is one in which sharp concern for curriculum is being shown in several quarters: it is not always the official voice of central or of local government which is loudest. Parents and employers as well as teachers and their pupils are expected to understand and to be to some degree enlightened.

Anyone who has a part to play in managing change within curriculum has to be aware of the history and of the traditions which have shaped what we now have. Without this awareness the manager is likely not to notice some useful lessons from the past. He is also likely to allow old-fashioned distortions of an idea to go unnoticed. In short, he needs the sophistication which knowledge and a sense of time can give him.

Because curriculum has developed in a manner which has taken human, political, professional and economic sensitivities into account, the lessons for the management of present-day change in England should have significance for those societies where the history of curriculum is shorter, or more derivative, or so centralised that flexibility and change has in the past been a matter of edict rather than of professional and public participation.

As a beginning, the notion of curriculum change in the educational system of England and Wales will be examined. Attention will be paid to the inheritance of influences under which we now work.

Origins of change

What a child learns will influence how he looks at life around him. If a state tries to control how people see the world rather than leave them to their own interpretation, curriculum is a useful instrument of control. It can, early on, indoctrinate and prescribe.

To indoctrinate is not always undemocratic or, in one sense, wicked.

When the United States of America were populated by first generations of heterogeneous immigrants, common school curricula were important instruments – and perhaps the only reliable ones – by which to attempt to unify the culture and to create a single history.

In a politically embattled state, on the other hand, a uniform view of the rest of the world is politically desirable; it creates loyalty and it promotes solidarity, pride in accepting one way of life and pity (or something worse) for another. A clear example of totalitarian curriculum can be seen in the Soviet Union; less clear are the examples of satellite states in Eastern Europe, where the memory of a free interpretation of the individual's view of the world sometimes clashes with a vision which is limited by political constraint.

In some ways nineteenth century Britain resembled in its education the Eastern European states of the twentieth century. There were those who had dreams of an open society and there were others who recognised that class differences could not allow society to be free. There were visionaries and pragmatists, planners, enthusiasts and time-servers. In one way, each of these *almost* grasped the point that a curriculum could change a view, could affect an attitude, could create respect or conformity, could perpetuate a culture or lay the basis for something different; but no one quite succeeded in getting the point. This in itself is a major part of the history of English education.

It is not surprising that no one fully grasped one hundred and fifty years ago – or even a century back – that education is connected with the control of opinions and ideas and these themselves are connected with the shaping of society. It is not surprising that no one seemed fully to realise the political potency of education. Partly this is explained by a greater preoccupation with what was then morality than with politics, with church and with Sunday Schools rather than with secular education; partly it is accounted for by the lack of connection between theories about knowledge (which abounded in the nineteenth century and far earlier) and the practice of imparting knowledge. It was, again, too little realised how knowledge differs from attitude and how education differed in the way it could impart or affect either of these.

These seeming deficiencies in our forefathers' ways of thinking are, in hindsight, easy to spot. It would, however, in their time have been immeasurably difficult to imagine a system of truly popular education or an effortless way of communicating uniform ideas of the kind to which we are now accustomed. Because of this, it would have been almost inconceivable to plan a wide scale system of uniform teacher-education, to assume broadly comparable expectations on the part of parents in differing towns, regions or even parishes of England.

It would have been almost impossible, in brief, to see that education had anything to do with larger purposes than the teaching of simple skills.

Character, morals, social behaviour, kindness and good manners were matters for the home – and whether the home was effective or not was not really society's concern. How you looked at the world was determined by your station in life – and that in turn was decided, first, by accidents of birth and then by seemingly less accidental factors of class and money.

Early on, there were many other forces which could give shape to those things which we nowadays expect to be influenced by school curriculum. Because of this, curriculum was something which was left to be more or less glimpsed, simply, from the corner of officialdom's eye. It was something incidental or marginal. It was so little concerned with education in itself that its shape was affected by considerations of economy and administration far more than by ideas about upbringing or about learning.

If we want evidence of the almost incidental way in which, in the very early days of state education in England and Wales, matters affecting the curriculum were treated, we can trace how the influence of central government in education grew in some areas and dwindled in others. This is very clearly depicted in, for instance, Dr A. S. Bishop's *The rise of a central authority for English education* (1971). He points out, as an example, why it is that we have a long and official tradition of greater interest for the buildings of schools rather than for what goes on inside them. Treasury Minutes of 1833, 1834, and 1835 had laid down regulations for financial grants for education. Those rules were concerned only with school fabric; they entered into detail about who should pay how big a proportion, how accounts should be audited and so on; they revealed, too, that a preference – which seems to have lingered for a long time in the relationship of central to local government – should be shown for large towns and cities in the payment of any grant. Indeed in 1864 *The Saturday Review* could say that there was imprinted on half the rural parishes of the country 'a deep conviction that the Education Department is their natural enemy, whom it is their first duty to elude, baffle and disprove to the utmost of their power'.

The need to pay out financial grants led, in education as in other publicly administered services, to the construction of complicated sets of rules. Money had to be distributed equitably, honestly and regularly. This meant that regulations grew in number and that they were increasingly careful, refined and restrictive. As they became more sophisticated, these regulations moved further and further away from the purposes which they were originally intended to serve.

At first, the payment of grant was concerned with the erection and maintenance of schools; schools were intended to provide education. Education, however, was fairly soon found to be a long way from the spirit of any regulation; about two decades after the first Treasury Minutes, the manner in which grants were made was examined in detail.

The administrative machinery of the Department of Education was scrutinised. The Newcastle Commission was established in the summer of 1858 to enquire into the state of popular education in England. It confirmed the suspicions of those who had urged its setting up; in particular there had been a fear lest a group of mere officials should be responsible, without proper accountability, for spending large sums of public money while elementary schools – such as they were – drifted into the position of finding themselves under centralised but purposeless government control.

The Duke of Newcastle's enquiry had to include in its work recommendations about the extension of 'sound and cheap elementary instruction to all classes of the people'. Not surprisingly, the enquiry uncovered the fact that the Department of Education was not capable of bringing about this extension. It employed an administrative machine which was overloaded to the point of almost seizing up: 'a great evil in the amount of work has been ... that the office has been so absorbed by the day's work that there has been very little time to consider what improvements might be made in the education system'.

It emerged, of course, that the Education Department at Whitehall was trying to control all manner of minute and unimportant things. The justification for indulging in very small-scale bureaucracy was the usual one of the fear of mismanagement and fraud. Not unnaturally the Newcastle Commission felt that the burden should be eased. In trying to decide how it should be eased it had to avoid risks of fraudulence, protect the Treasury from excessive claims and, in a moment of imagination, encourage local interest in education. The best way out would have been to establish local school boards. But the time was too early; the idea of paying a grant to the board of managers of each school according to the quality of its children's school attainment was introduced instead.

What became known as the Revised Code for the conduct of schools (1862) stemmed from this: its evils have been frequently documented. The Newcastle Commission had made it clear that in even the best of elementary schools only a very small group of children could reach the top of the school. At the top level, children were well taught. Below the top group, however, the majority of children received only a very imperfect education. 'The Commissioners held that the time had come when a further attempt should be made to influence the instruction of the large body of inferior schools which had hitherto been little affected. They proposed to do this by offering distinct inducements to the masters of all schools to bring their pupils to a certain mark' (Hadow Report (1931), *Report of the Consultative Committee on the Primary School*).

The Newcastle recommendation was one of the earliest to affect curriculum in broad terms. What is significant is that in those early days it was standard of attainment rather than content which seemed to matter more. In response to Newcastle, the Revised Code instituted a system of six standards corresponding to the six years of school life between the end of the infant stage and the age of twelve years.

Grants could not be earned by children over the age of twelve. Teachers therefore concentrated on teaching the three rudimentary subjects of reading, writing and arithmetic (together, always, with needlework for girls) to younger pupils. Because the Code affected only those who were over the age of six years, infant pupils were only indirectly touched by its more drastic effects. Part of the success of British styles of infant education in the present day can be traced back to this.

But however easy it is to score off the seemingly unenlightened days of the 1860s, at the Revised Code, at payment by results, at the predominance of the three Rs, there were nevertheless benefits.

The Code, even apart from a beneficial outcome in secularising the instruction of state schools, was skilful in the gradings that it asked for; this much was borne out by the Board of Education's report, through a consultative committee, on *Psychological Tests of Educable Capacity* (1924). Teachers were not asked to do the impossible. 'When the mass of young illiterate children that formed the body of most schools had been passed through the first two standards, the remaining requirements of the Code could be fulfilled at the cost of reasonably hard work, except in schools with inadequate staffs, bad attendance, or a very poor class of children.' What was wrong about the Revised Code was that at the time of its introduction one or all of these disadvantages affected the majority of schools.

But it should also be acknowledged that when teachers were placed in the position of having to make individual bargains and contracts with local managers, they lost security and rights which they otherwise enjoyed when they were directly governed – as to payment of grant for their salary – from London. Nevertheless the substitution of managers' arrangements in the end created an advantage. Teachers lost their status as civil servants; in fact they moved, after the Newcastle Report, naturally into the world of local government. In turn, when they became full employees of local authorities British teachers enjoyed a freedom which they would not have enjoyed under central government and which their counterparts in some other countries still do not enjoy. The teacher's curricular freedom was not an intended benefit: its origins lay in bureaucratic failure.

This failure lay in the ineptitude of the Board of Education (as it was then called) to win between 1902 and 1918 the control over school affairs which it sought busily and deviously through the imposition of model Articles of Government and Management upon schools which had been taken over by

Local Education Authorities. The battle was full of bureaucratic tedium and had little direct impact on education. Nevertheless those in local authority associations and those in the teacher associations themselves fought hard. They resisted the idea that any model – however good it might seem – should be imposed upon local freedom. This allows those who now teach in schools in England and Wales to claim a freedom and to boast an autonomy which few others possess.

But another benefit also lay in the days of the Revised Code of the three Rs and of payment by results. This second benefit can be seen in the way it allowed schools to move away from testing children in denominational affairs to seeking some evidence of their attainment in secular learning. By attaching the payment of central government grant only to attainments in basic subjects, the emphasis on religious teaching could be undermined in schools. There had, early in the nineteenth century, been some determination to rid the denominational system of what many considered to be one of its less defensible features, among which was what was described as 'the petty proselytizing of pupils against the wishes of their parents'. The Revised Code, whatever else its iniquities might have been, made things easier for an ultimate reconciliation between secular and denominational ideas. It meant that secular curriculum could assume the importance which had earlier been denied to it.

The idea of making it a universal necessity to reach a minimum of educational attainment was as attractive in the nineteenth century as it still is to some people. But the attempt to link grants and salaries to children's attainments was so heartily condemned that both central government and, later, local boards of education and local education authorities hesitated to burn their fingers a second time. By the end of the nineteenth century payment by results had, for one reason or another, created an inefficient mode of education, with large classes and low-paid teachers. Because qualified teachers were more expensive than anything else, a greater number of unqualified *instructors* were employed. All this was done in the name of economy. It was the first British attempt at introducing the idea of measurable efficiency into an unambitious nineteenth century curriculum.

Restrictions

The effects of the Revised Code's restrictions lasted some time. It was in their aftermath that the first major legislation (*The Elementary Education Act, 1870*) was passed. This made it obligatory to set up local School Boards in addition to having, simply, managers for each school. The Act too was intended to establish the idea of compulsory elementary schooling for everyone.

RESTRICTIONS

The activity of establishing School Boards was an engrossing one; it diverted national attention from the actual business of teaching for two decades or more. But in 1895 it was rediscovered that teachers and those outside schools did not necessarily agree about the process of education. It led to the beginning of an almost continuing dilemma about the definition of curriculum.

The dilemma consists in having to decide whether it is a matter which is imposed upon children for their greater good by those who are older (i.e. grown-up) or whether the curriculum should serve their needs – whether these be intellectual or emotional or physical. In the early days the conundrum was expressed with some subtlety – but in a way which does less justice than we would nowadays pay to nuances of words about the freedom of teachers. It was, for instance, said that there was a well-marked distinction of intellectual attitude: on the one side, professional scholastic opinion was on the whole fearful of local authorities and inclined to propose that they should be, if not muzzled, yet so constituted and conditioned as to be made as innocuous as possible; on the other side, what we may term as the administrative and political mind looked hopefully to such authorities as the most potent and promising factors for the solution of the problem.

Each attidude is explicable enough. The schoolmaster, the more competent he is and the more assured in position, wants the more to be let alone. What he needs in order to attain the best results is 'on the one side, command of means and possession of pupils, and, on the other, freedom of hand and method; and so he desires what he conceives to be the simple conditions of success'. But the administrator sees the other side of the question – the necessity of creating and maintaining the machinery which the schoolmaster has to work, and he knows that this can best be done by evoking popular interest and allowing parental or family care for posterity to inspire the educational work and agencies of the present. It was felt that it would be a serious evil if education were allowed to become the business of the schoolmaster alone; it could be claimed that '. . . the more completely it grows into the concern of the whole people, and is made a part of their common life and civil policy, the more it will flourish, the better it will become'.

These words were used by a famous administrator in a little known report (the Bryce Report) which made recommendations about the best methods of establishing a well-organised system of education in England. Confusion had still grown about who was responsible for each part of education. There was the central Education Department, there were newly established counties or county boroughs (1889) and there were many differing ways in which grants for education were administered. The Bryce Report led to the establishment in 1899 of a national Board of Education which took over the Education Department, The Science and Art Department, and the educational aspects of the work of the Charity Commission. Even then, confusions remained: secondary education was too far separated from elementary education. It was not until 1901 that School Boards were entitled by statute to spend money on secondary education, that is for children over the age of twelve. This was the result of what was known as the Cockerton Judgement, when the decision of a government auditor to disallow expenditure by the London School Board on post-elementary education was upheld by the Court of Appeal. A special regulation had to be passed to permit School Boards to spend money on secondary education. It was a temporary measure which tided things over until the 1902 Act which, it was known, would impose a proper order on earlier confusions. It was then that a first glimmer was visible of what a systematic curriculum might be.

In what it had said about the teacher's freedom, the Bryce Report painted a picture which is familiar three-quarters of a century later. Tension about curriculum between the teacher and the administrator of education still exists in Britain. The tension may, as we shall see later, now lack some reality. But the assumption or even the pretence that it still exists is sometimes helpful to administrators and teachers who wish to avoid a clash. It is, regrettably, even more helpful to those who in the field of administration find it easier to pretend that their professionalism excludes any direct concern for education *per se*. James Bryce, in fact, defined the situation as we know it today. What he said signalled an advance in thinking about public education; it has been echoed in every subsequent national report about education.

But in whatever way things later turned out, by the time that Local Education Authorities took over from the School Boards, tension about curriculum between those inside schools and those who were outside was clearly marked. The introduction of the 1902 Education Bill for the establishment of LEAs included references which were disparaging to the teacher. 'To the educationist ... I need make no apologies and offer no excuses ... He has long seen a vast expenditure of public money which has left this country far behind all its continental and American rivals in matters of education.' In introducing the Bill the Prime Minister, Mr Balfour, also spoke of the need to spend a 'huge average cost per pupil in our elementary schools and yet at the same time ... many of these schools are half-starved, inadequately equipped, and imperfectly staffed'.

This note of dissatisfaction did not prevent the 1902 Education Act from giving the national Board of Education considerable titular powers – through the drawing up of codes of regulation and through the system of school inspection. But if these gave some degree of *control* over what went on in schools, it gave the Board no power to initiate. The new Local Education Authorities could move forward, in curriculum as well as in matters which affected the internal organisation of schools, at whatever pace they wished.

RESTRICTIONS

This marked the end of one of the first stages in curriculum development in Britain. Successive periods were to witness the renewed influence of tests and examinations on curriculum. These were destined to be different from the effect of payment by results. Tests were not to be used as a means of securing any national standardisation of attainment. They were, instead, going to be used to select children for different types of education. In this they can be identified with the type of limitation within which curriculum has had to be developed in the last half of this century.

2 Who should be in charge of curriculum?

We have already seen that the Bryce Report posed the problem of whether it should be those within schools or the users of education – the employers, the parents and the children themselves – who should have the major voice in determining what should happen. It was not seriously thought at that time that the teacher was properly competent to make autonomous decisions about the education of his charges. Not surprisingly, the Board of Education was inclined, in the early days, to think of curriculum in a very straightforward way. It was not, admittedly required that the teacher should obey regulation; nevertheless he was formally expected to accept guidance – and without question. The distinction between requirement and guidance, between prescription and expectation has been something which has befogged the idea of a developing curriculum through many generations. It is worth briefly examining how confusions arose.

In the early days guidance was given in plenty by both the Board of Education and by the Local Education Authorities. Because trained teachers were still in short supply, guidance given by experts was important. It covered, even from the beginning, both elementary and secondary education.

Because the curriculum of elementary and secondary schools was thought to differ in nature as well as in difficulty or complexity, it seems important that we should understand quite how elementary and secondary education was supposed to differ.

At the very beginning of the century there had existed Higher Grade Board Schools and a small number of Higher Elementary Schools. Many of the former were converted after the 1902 Act into separate secondary schools. In addition there were in some areas Central Schools, which gave full-time education to some children up to the age of fifteen and in which the curriculum was designed to enable them to enter trade or industry after leaving school.

Elsewhere there were Day Trade Schools and Junior Technical Schools, each narrower in their vocational purpose. But in its Regulations for Secondary Schools in 1907 the Board of Education required local education authorities to arrange for secondary schools (whose curriculum was on the whole broad and non-vocational) to make available 25 per cent of their places as Free Places. This meant that pupils who applied for admission and

WHO SHOULD BE IN CHARGE OF CURRICULUM?

who passed an entrance test of attainment and efficiency were educated without the payment of a fee. One effect of this, according to the Hadow Report on the Primary School (1931) was that teachers began to devote more attention to the instruction of children under the age of eleven years in order to bring them up to the standard of what came to be called the Free Place entrance tests.

The 1931 Report commented on the curriculum of younger children. It pointed out that in many places infant schools preceded the elementary schools. It was impossible not to be struck by the contrast between the rather arid and narrow conception of education as conducted in the monitorial schools (that is, schools in which older pupils were themselves taught and were in turn set to teach others), in which the instruction was almost entirely limited to the three Rs, with needlework for girls, and in some instances a little gardening and other occupations for the boys, and the comparatively rich tradition underlying the curriculum provided in the better infant schools.

An example of the post-infant curriculum can be found in the revised (1937) edition of the *Handbook of Suggestions for Teachers in Public Elementary Schools*. There it was suggested that in every public elementary school a definite course of work should be mapped out for the children to follow. The timetable should usually show it as divided up into a number of subjects and activities. The Handbook admitted that the curriculum thus represented had arisen in a somewhat haphazard way. It had in most cases no philosophical basis and could not be said to have evolved organically. It began as a simple combination of religion, needlework and the three Rs; new subjects had been added from time to time under pressure from public opinion.

The introduction of each new subject caused a certain amount of dislocation in the existing curriculum and a great deal of argument and heart-burning about the time to be given to the old and the new. It was thought natural, nevertheless, that a new subject should be thought about as to its purpose. Were children to learn additional subjects in order that they might acquire fresh knowledge? Were they to be exposed to new ideas for the more or less abstract training of their mind – without any necessary relation between this and the needs of a vocationally directed world? Were children simply to be exposed to new cultural experiences in the hope that this would give them breadth and a deeper understanding of the ways in which the heritage of English education might enrich their future lives?

Questions like these have, of course, always been central to the argument about breadth versus specialisation and they have always been questions which have been difficult to answer in arguments which centre on the purposes of education: is curriculum something which fits a child out in a useful way to earn his living or is it, instead, something which simply meets his childishly maturing needs?

The debate about these two ways of looking at curriculum always seem to be argued more fiercely in terms of secondary school education than in connection with the schooling of younger children. Even in 1904 it had, for instance, been insisted that in secondary schools instruction should be general, that is, it should be such as would give a reasonable degree of exercise and development for the whole of a child's faculties. It should not confine development to a particular channel, whether that of pure and applied science or of literary and linguistic study, or of that kind of acquirement which was directed at fitting a boy or a girl to better work in a subordinate capacity.

The idea that those who left 'ordinary' secondary schools would always have to enter work in a so-called subordinate capacity may strike us nowadays as strange. But in the terms of the early twentieth century there was a type of Mr Kipps inevitability about the way in which you started at the bottom of the ladder, worked your way slowly (and with a certain amount of good fortune) to some higher rung. What happened at school was merely an activity which enabled you to put a foot on the very first of those rungs of human advancement which the world of commerce and of industry understood better than any mere school teacher.

Amongst those who tried to define the purposes of curriculum in the early days it was accepted that specialisation – and here one assumes that they always meant specialisation by subject rather than specialisation in terms of vocational purpose – should begin only after a so-called general education had been carried to the point at which '. . . the habit of exercising all faculties had been formed'. On this kind of philosophy it was assumed that a certain solid basis for life could be laid. Much would depend on the child's acquaintance with the structure and laws of the physical world, with his accuracy in the use of thought and language, and on his practical ability to begin dealing with affairs of the world.

In themselves ideas such as these – and which are taken from official statements of the objectives of schooling in the period immediately after the establishment of local education authorities – have a thoughtful and sincere sound to them. It was insisted that those who entered secondary schools should complete a course of instruction which was whole: this meant that the course which each child followed had to be planned so as to lead up to a clear standard of acquirement in a variety of branches of instruction. The last thing that was wanted was that children should stop short at some merely superficial introduction to any subject. Thoroughness, hard work, clearly stated standards of attainment – each of these typified the approach to curriculum which dominated not only the first part of the present century but also much of the thinking which has persisted to the present day.

We have admittedly moved away from the idea that schools should be of different types and that each type should be suited to the differing requirements of pupils, to the place of those pupils in the social organisation of our country, to the means and the wealth of their parents, and to the age at which the regular education of pupils would be obliged to stop short. We have become accustomed to the idea that children may go on being educated regardless of whether their earning capacity will be helpful to their homes.

Social arrangements have changed to such an extent that we are able to look at the curriculum as something which goes well beyond the mere days of formal schooling. Nevertheless, one of the more serious questions which has to be asked about the management of curriculum change in the present day is whether we are fully sensitive to the idea that curriculum is something which has a degree of continuity from the days which precede the child's entry into school as an infant through to the permanent education, the life-long education which we feel the educative process should entail.

Certainly those who are responsible for the design and management of curriculum are nowadays free of presumptions about the social class of their pupils or students, about whether or not their parents can afford to keep them in education, and about the way in which our society will have marked certain people out for certain positions of superiority, of command, of inferiority, or of service regardless of their own innate capacities. The development of democratic ideals about the nature of the human beings and about the ways in which we are to be educated has led to the acceptance that each person has within himself a distinct personal identity and authority and it has, equally, led to the acceptance of service as something which each one of us owes to the community in which we live and work. Idealistic though this may sound, one of the more optimistic marks of latter-day curriculum management has been the assumption that curriculum is something which has a relevance for life in its broadest aspects and not to the more narrowly defined assumptions which led to earlier statements of guidance about teaching, educating and the making of curricula.

Where does responsibility lie?

Only the social historian can tell us about those forces within our communities which gave to certain people the right to act as the interpreters or the dictators of curriculum in the early part of this century. Certainly there was no attempt to conceal presuppositions about the way in which curriculum was meant to preserve social division.

Comparably there was no concealment about the way in which the apparent openness of education in England and Wales was to be administratively controlled to the point where even the number of minutes in the day which were allocated to this part of the curriculum or to that were to be dictated by somebody who knew better than the class teacher herself. For instance, not less than four-and-a-half hours a week were to be devoted to English, Geography and History; not less than three-and-a-half hours per week were to be devoted to language, nor less than seven-and-a-half hours to science and mathematics. Despite this very tight control it could still be claimed in official documents that ample time was left in what was described as a well-planned curriculum for additions to be made to these minimum requirements so as to include adequate provision for systematic physical exercises, for drawing, for singing, for manual training, and for the instruction of girls in the elements of housewifery and '. . . for such other subjects as might profitably be included in the curriculum of any particular school'.

In the midst of so many seemingly reasonable demands upon his time the teacher could hardly have been blamed for feeling that his own part in determining the curriculum which his pupils might need was negligible. The teacher stood in the middle of the battle, the purposes of which he perhaps understood only partly: the battle lay between the Board of Education and the new local education authorities. Had it been possible for the Board of Education to retain control over what went on within the maintained schools of England and Wales, then the prescriptions laid down by Manuals of Guidance, Handbooks of Suggestions and the rest of them, might have carried not simply persuasiveness but also real authority. As things happened, however, the local education authorities were quite properly conscious of the fact that they themselves had been entrusted by statute with the efficient running of their schools. One effect of the acceptance of this responsibility was that there were local manuals of guidance and local handbooks of suggestions which competed, to some extent, with those which emanated from London.

The teacher, with a still very recent memory of the tests, standards, requirements and procedures which had been laid down in order to establish proficiency and expertness, not unnaturally paid a great deal of attention to those things which other people said about the curriculum. It is not at all surprising that the early years of the century witnessed an ever increasing tendency to name specific subjects which had, in one way or another, to find their place in the curriculum. Subjects as such belonged more to the field of secondary education; with comparable insidiousness, however, demands were made upon a variety of *activities* which would be included in the school day for the younger child. The infants' school had, as has already been said, been remarkably free of the pressures of distortion. Behind the apparent liberalism of the education of young children, however, lay the same demand that a course of instruction should be complete and should be planned so as to lead up to a standard of acquirement.

In 1905 the original edition of *A Handbook of Suggestions for Teachers in Public Elementary Schools* told schools that the only uniformity of practice that the Board of Education wished to see was that every teacher should think for himself and should work out for himself such methods of teaching as would use his powers to the best advantage. It was also added that in this way it was hoped that the capacity of teachers would be best suited to the particular needs and conditions of individual schools. It was denied that uniformity in detail of practice – apart from the mere routine of school management – was in any way desirable; it was even denied that such uniformity might be attainable. Nevertheless the moral was driven home quite hard – any freedom which the teacher might acquire from this line of reasoning would imply a corresponding responsibility in the use of that freedom.

Although, then, the teacher was taking part in a conflict which he did not fully understand, there were two influences at work: the one was influence which we could describe as political. The battle between the Board of Education and the new local education authorities could be claimed to have led the Board to the point of doing one of two things. It could either lay down a form of government which would ensure the type of uniformity which would secure comparability of standard, of method, and of the content of curriculum throughout England and Wales, or, alternatively, it could deny a comparable power of influence to the local education authorities. It could do this by insisting that true professionalism for the teacher meant that he should make up his own mind. The second major influence which was at work on curriculum was not a personal one; it was connected wholly with professionalism in itself – and not simply with professionalism as a catchword.

Most of the official literature of the time (which seizes on this rather than upon the procedural, administrative, and more political aspects of curriculum) reads with as much truth as it would in the present day. Essentially the professionalism of the teacher in deciding upon the appropriate curriculum for his pupils is concerned not with subjects but with what were then known – and remained with the same title for many years – as activities.

The type of thing that was written in guidance for the teacher stressed the need for right attitudes. It was emphasised that the teachers should know their children and should sympathise with them for it was '... of the essence of teaching that the mind of the teacher should touch the mind of the pupil'. It was assumed that the teacher would at each stage adjust his mind to that of his pupil, that he would draw upon his pupils' experience as a supplement to his own, and that he would '... as it were take them into partnership for the acquisition of knowledge'.

Very little that will be written in the 1970s could improve upon this as the description of the way in which the teacher has responsibility in England and Wales for the design and management of curriculum.

Part of Britain's good fortune in enjoying a continuity of respect for the teacher in control of the curriculum rests upon the work of those early psychologists who stressed that the attention which children gave to their learning should be exhibited not in isolation but in relation to their own past experience. It was accepted that each lesson should be a renewal and an increase of what was described as 'a connected store of experience'. This store of experience in turn became a body of knowledge.

This view of the teacher's responsibility had a high-minded ring to it; the kind of language which was used in order to reinforce the message of the teacher's personal responsibility towards his pupils was full of phrases such as the need to impress upon children the dignity of knowledge, the duty to use personal powers to the best advantage, and 'the truth that life is a serious as well as a pleasant thing'.

New and traditional responsibilities

The three traditional influences on those who made the decisions about curriculum were, then, political, utilitarian and moral. In one degree or another each of these made a demand upon the teacher not always as the autonomous, professional person we now expect him to be. Nevertheless, in each aspect the teacher was expected to make a response which was serious-minded, well-intentioned, and devoted to the good of his pupils.

By the 1970s three further aspects had been added to the responsibilities which had to be taken into account when a teacher – or anyone else – makes a decision about the management of curriculum. Nowadays the nature of democracy is defined rather differently. The soft jargon of participation, the conception that human dignity involves certain kinds of rights, and that each man has a certain type of freedom to choose how to benefit himself, or how to act to his own disadvantage – each of these carries a potency today which it did not in the early part of the century.

Secondly, a new idea exists about the usefulness of education. It is not enough that we should be able to insist that the principal concerns of education are those of improving the spiritual status of man or that we have some singular right to pay attention to his moral needs, or that we are in the unique position, through education, to do something for the enhancement of his life which other aspects of social activity are incapable of providing. This may amount to saying no more than that the present-day view of education is a pragmatic one. Education must provide personal satisfaction, but amongst these personal satisfactions it must recognise that it also has to pay off.

A third set of ideas affects education more clearly nowadays. It would surprise our Edwardian predecessors to hear us claim that the idea of change, of progress, and of rapidity of improvement were of greater concern to us now than these ideas were to them. Without relaxing into a kind of language which evokes phrases such as 'the explosion of knowledge', it is obvious that there is nowadays more to be learned, that what is to be learned increases with a frightening rapidity, and that we have great uncertainty about the kind of knowledge, the kind of personal adjustment, and the type of overall world outlook which is needed by those who are now young if they are to face the next century with competence and calmness.

The principal disadvantage which faces the manager of curriculum development against the background of these three additional sets of factors – and there are likely to be many more – is the absence of authoritative guidance. Nothing from the Department of Education and Science, nothing from the local education authorities, from Institutes of Education, from professional associations, or from research institutes can provide the same type of certainty about interpretation as was available in the past. This means that to carry responsibility for making choices about curriculum is to move in the dark. Admittedly each of us has companions in this darkness – but we lack the certainty that we know enough or can find out enough to be clear, either in our own minds or to be able to influence other people in sufficient time to make good choices about future curriculum.

A fourth, and less diffuse, uncertainty lies behind responsibility for making new curriculum. In the beginning of this century official reports, manuals of guidance, handbooks and exhortations to shape the child's education suffered from self-contradiction. There was far less certainty then than there is now about the difference between instruction and education, far less was known about the acquisition of knowledge, about the place of attitudes and motivation. There were different views of life at large and it was perhaps not understood that curriculum was something more than a collection of subjects or a collection of activities.

The confusion of those who in the early days had authority for creating curriculum was made rather worse because a major transition was then occurring in English education, between elementary education for everyone and secondary education for some. The philosophy of how far secondary education should become universal was full of confusion. This confusion has at least been removed. For the past thirty or forty years England and Wales have been accustomed to the idea that secondary education up to the age of the mid-teens should be a universal right for every child.

This one element of certainty should give us the confidence to be able to plan a curriculum which extends from the age of five to the age at least of sixteen and possibly to the age of eighteen or nineteen. We no longer need waste energy on deciding whether there are differing types of children in our schools and whether for that reason different types of curricula are needed. We are free from the wasteful and enervating task of trying to describe some children as being brighter and others more dull, others as being younger, others more old, and because of this as having different or more serious or better defined purposes for their curriculum. Certainly the differences between children in our schools are becoming better known. More clearly we see that individual needs differ. This child's pace differs from the speed with which that child can work. This child's level of motivation differs from that child's wish to learn. The language of individualised learning is something which is only now beginning to become clear.

We are not certain how ideas and experiments about individual learning programmes – which involve theory of learning as well as a great deal of highly complicated information about the psychology of learning – can catch up with decisions about the *design* of curriculum. It may be that to think about the methods by which children learn and to think about the design and development of curriculum are inseparable educational activities. On the other hand, it could be argued that the individualisation of learning is basically a matter of the personal psychology of children and that curriculum is a matter of school organisation. The first is about why I want to learn, when I want to learn, and about the speed with which I want to learn. The second is a matter about who it is that is to make choices for me, who is to offer me this teacher or that teacher, or this book or that other resource with which to promote the facility which I have for learning within this discipline or within that subject area.

Summary

In trying to answer the question of who should be in charge of the curriculum we have seen that official attempts to take control of something which we nowadays without question accept as belonging to the school failed at a comparatively early stage.

In Chapter 1 we saw that the very first attempts at creating some form of official and secular control of schooling were in the end beneficial to the cause of mass education. That there were failures and disappointments, and that there were misjudgements as well as pieces of tactlessness in the way in which central control was handled should not be taken as the principal reason for the system of schooling in England and Wales moving away in its entirety towards autonomy for the individual teacher. Who it is that designs the curriculum of our children is the teacher – or so we allege. That the teacher has this freedom has been a matter not of broad, enlightened or

SUMMARY

highly liberal policy but a series of results from mistakes, ill-judged conflicts and belated realisations of the nature of the educational process.

Who now controls curriculum is a question which is answered partly by referring to the three principal assumptions which existed in 1904, through 1918, through the 1930s and into the 1944 period and beyond. These assumptions basically had to do with the responsibility of the individual teacher, with the needs of children, and to some extent with the expectations which society expressed for curriculum as a whole. Nowadays there are at least three additional assumptions which have to be taken into account. These have been described; it has been made clear that there is no one source of authoritative resolution for our new problems. The questions are neither easy to ask nor easy to interpret. We do not even know whom to approach as a possible interpreter of the conundrums which mass technology, a very rapid speed of change and very marked differences in what is expected of education now amount to.

The manager of curriculum development needs the same kind of certainty about new problems as his predecessor could rely upon when the openness of our educational system was less noticeable than it now is. Later chapters will suggest the sources of help to which we may nowadays turn in managing something which seems so completely new as to be either unconvincing or totally mysterious. First, however, it is necessary to unravel the effect of the design of curriculum which has always been felt in England and Wales from one known and particular source – that of examinations. Examinations, both for younger and for older children, have, in this country as in others, had an unavoidable effect upon the design of the ways in which we expect children to learn. It is nowadays fashionable to assert that examinations are constricting, that they create a need to specialise on certain choices of subject too early, that they are unreliable, and that even if their principal effects relate only to the late teenager, nevertheless their influence is felt much lower in the age range.

Examinations and assessment very crudely intermingle to create the one single system of measurement which any developed educational system can enjoy. Examinations tell children how they are succeeding or failing; they give comparable information to teachers. Examinations also tell those who pay for education what they are getting for their money. The parent, the employer, the tax-payer, and the user of education, each of these has a stake in the continuity of examinations and in their efficiency. It is only natural, therefore, that in a system where competition, achievement and the need to accredit, qualify and to sort people out for varying jobs at differing ages – that all this should have a very considerable effect upon the way in which children are educated. It is not a matter of regret that examinations have such a positive effect upon curriculum. The puzzle is that it has taken so long

WHO SHOULD BE IN CHARGE OF CURRICULUM?

to see that examinations and curriculum are bound together not in an unholy way but in a wedlock which should prove fruitful. The following chapter will examine the eugenic effect of examinations.

3 Examinations and the curriculum

Although the wish to reform education had been strongly expressed from time to time and although it had been expressed both from within and outside the classroom, the strongest influence on the curriculum had been exercised by the examination system of England and Wales.

In their origins in the nineteenth century public examinations had had several good effects; the principles of patronage and religious tests had given way to the idea that entry to public services should be allowed on the basis of merit as revealed in written examination. The Home and the Indian Civil Service, Oxford and Cambridge, the Royal Military Academy at Woolwich, the University of London – all these became accessible in the mid-century through the doorway of examinations. Gladstone himself is reported to have commented on the introduction of examinations, that they would allow the lazy doctrine that men are much of a muchness to give way to something which would amount to a much higher respect for merit and to a more effectual standard of competence. Gladstone, too, had an unusual view of competitiveness. He had never been particularly successful in competitive situations but nevertheless he felt that after passing from a period of prerogative to patronage and from a period of bribery to influence, it was natural that progress should not end there. He cherished, as he put it, the hope that the day would be near at hand when it would be both practical and economical in the improvement of human affairs for the State 'to accept a new and striking sign of rational confidence in the intelligence and character of people'.

This political-cum-philosophic view of examinations and of their benefit in time had its effect upon the curriculum of schools. Severe examinations were established for honours bachelor degrees at Oxford and Cambridge; it is claimed that these had a salutary, if indirect, influence on the teaching of the principal disciplines (classics and mathematics) in the ancient grammar schools and public schools. In the same way the establishment at Cambridge of the Natural Science Tripos in 1851 and of the Honours School of Natural Science at Oxford in 1853 did comparable good in preparing the way for the inclusion of science in the curriculum of schools.

Another benefit from the Victorian introduction of public examinations was felt very urgently in the education of girls. It was accepted that from the inception of the movement of higher education of women the preparation of girls for examinations was a saving feature of a new form of schooling. This was because the admission of girls and women into public examinations came at a crucial moment in the reform of women's education; secondly, the preparation of women for examinations was the principal reason for the foundation of several important educational institutions which were exclusively devoted to their needs. Thirdly, in the view of the educational world in the nineteenth century and in the view of too many of the pioneers of women's education, a girl's capacity to pass examinations was the principal – if not the sole – criterion of educability. A fourth reason for the importance of examinations for girls was they provided a motive to study and they offered an inducement to parents to keep girls in full-time education.

Dissatisfaction with examinations

Despite the early benefits of examinations, both schools and the Board of Education expressed displeasure from about the beginning of the twentieth century. Examinations and in particular the School Certificate had good effects in bringing weak schools up to some respectable standards of teaching. But this, it was admitted, was not what examinations were designed for. Because it was generally regarded as the finishing line for the majority of sixteen year old pupils in school, the School Certificate had the effect of stereotyping and of narrowing the curriculum. The number of subjects which were studied at school became artificially limited. The curriculum became arid. Teaching became dull.

In a memorandum on *The Curricula of Secondary Schools* which the Board of Education published in 1913 as Circular 286 – and which the Spens Report twenty-five years later took very seriously – it was accepted that secondary schools had a twofold function: they were to provide a general preliminary education for those who aimed at occupations or professions requiring a highly trained intelligence and who meant to carry on their educational preparation for life to what was described as a considerably later age. They were also intended to provide for the education of a very large number of pupils who would leave school at or about the age of sixteen and who, contemplating no further full-time education, would at once proceed '... to posts in public offices, commercial houses and manufactories, or enter upon such occupations as farming and retail trade'.

The education of the first of these groups was inevitably and from the beginning affected by the demands of examinations. Up until 1943 it was possible to think of the potential university candidate as being part of a very separate category. In that year a report on curriculum and examinations (The Norwood Report) recommended that to meet the requirements of university entrance, of entry into the professions and to meet other needs, a School Leaving Examination should be conducted twice a year for pupils at 18+. Students would, in this examination, take the subjects required for their own particular purposes. The examination's own purpose (if indeed it had a separate purpose in itself) was *not* to provide evidence of a general or all-round education. This denial is both significant and, in its implications for curriculum, alarming.

The education of those who were to leave school at about sixteen was also influenced by examination syllabuses. These dated back to a period before 1911, when a Consultative Committee on Examinations in Secondary Schools reported to the Board of Education. The effects of examination requirements on the teacher were summarised then in words which seem likely to remain as a classic statement:

> 'The good effects of well-conducted examinations upon the teacher are that
> - they induce him to treat his subject thoroughly;
> - they make him so arrange his lessons as to cover with intellectual thoroughness a prescribed course of study within appointed limits of time;
> - they impel him to pay attention not only to his best pupils, but also to the backward and the slower amongst those who are being prepared for the examination;
> - they make him acquainted with the standard with other teachers and their pupils are able to reach in the same subject in other places of education.'

This recognisable defence was, however, counter-balanced:

> 'The effects of examinations on the teacher are *bad* insofar as
> - they constrain him to watch the examiner's foibles and to note his idiosyncrasies (or the tradition of the examination) in order that he may arm his pupils with the kind of knowledge required for dealing successfully with the questions that will probably be put to them;
> - they limit the freedom of the teacher in choosing the way in which he shall treat his subject;
> - they encourage him to take upon himself work which had better be left to the largely unaided efforts of his pupils, causing him to impart information to them in too digested a form or to select for them groups of facts or aspects of the subject which each pupil should properly be left to collect or envisage for himself;
> - they predispose the teacher to overvalue among his pupils that type of mental development which secures success in examinations;

– they make it the teacher's interest to excel in the purely examinable side of his professional work and divert his attention from those parts of education which cannot be tested by the process of examination.'

The evils outweighed the benefits; the evils were the greater because examinations were not centrally regulated. There were many different types of test for many specific purposes.

Simplification of examinations came with the introduction of the School Certificate and the Higher School Certificate in 1917. These were administered by a new governmental body (The Secondary Schools Examination Council) and they were successful for a time in checking the excesses of examination influence. By 1938, however, the Spens Report recorded that 'despite all safeguards, the School Certificate ... now dominates the work of schools, controlling both the framework and the content of curriculum.'

The ill-effects were at that time probably most noticeable among older pupils. In its Report for 1926–7 the Board of Education had commented on reports made by the Investigators of the Secondary Schools Examination Council about the suitability of the examinations for all types of pupils who remained at school between sixteen and eighteen years of age; they had commented that the Higher School Certificate was too specialised in character to meet the needs of the large and increasing number of pupils who stayed on at school after taking the First Examination but did not intend to proceed to a university. This view was, they felt, supported by the opinion that a considerable number of candidates would have been better occupied in pursuing a less ambitious course of study than that demanded for the Higher Certificate Examination.

In 1935 the Annual Report used almost identical words with which to complain about the high degree of specialisation in the examination at eighteen. Things, however, went further this time: 'The Secondary Schools Examination Council consider that some modification of the examination is desirable and with the concurrence of the Board of Education have approved a proposal by the Northern Universities Joint Matriculation Board for a reduction in standard and a revision of syllabus required for each subject.'

Attempts to ease the worst effects of examinations on curriculum

For one examinations board to try to adjust standards and syllabuses was, as we can see in hindsight, unlikely to succeed. The real difficulty was caused by two major procedural requirements of the examination at the age of eighteen. First, the examination could only be taken successfully if pupils gave an adequate performance within specific groups of subjects. Secondly, schools had to present classes as a whole – and not individual pupils – for examination. Both of these regulations meant that examinations had a far deeper effect on secondary school curriculum than they would have had if single subject examinations had existed earlier and if individual pupils had been allowed to choose their own combination of subjects. It could certainly be claimed that examinations in grouped subjects and those for which whole classes had to be put forward gave a sense of direction to grammar school education. But it was a direction which the schools themselves did not choose. They might have chosen no better even had they been given the choice: but they were denied that very simple freedom.

Against this background the Norwood Report was revolutionary when it proposed, in place of an external examination, an internal one under the control of teachers and a single subject examination with a free choice of subjects rather than an examination in grouped subjects. The same report also recommended an examination at the age of sixteen which should not try to predict future academic performance. For that purpose, suggested Norwood, another and separate examination was needed.

All this sounds familiar: the Beloe Committee, acting in 1960 as a sub-committee of the Secondary Schools Examination Council, grasped every nettle that it could. It took over where the Norwood Report left off: there it had been proposed that seven years should elapse before a teacher-controlled examination should come into operation. The proposals by the Beloe Committee for the establishment of the new Certificate of Secondary Education had to wait only five years for implementation. A teacher-controlled, single subject examination designed to fit the needs of pupils in the upper 60 per cent of the ability range was to become available to schools. It could be examined at school rather than externally and the variety of choices as to mode of examination and type of syllabus was very open. (However, the most popular method of examining now that the new examination is well-established is, after all, the traditional one of externally set papers, externally marked; this may be a sufficient comment on the difficulty which teachers find in using legitimate freedoms.)

Admittedly CSE has released curriculum from some of the constraints which were noticed in 1911, 1926, 1935, and 1943. There is now no need for arbitrary and seemingly trivial choices to be made among a number of examining boards. What were regarded by teachers as insignificant factors dictated by outsiders need no longer shape what children should learn. There is no longer a need to strain continually to prove high standards by insisting on some irreducible difficulty in examination papers.

Something, thus, has been achieved. But what are left are problems of considerable severity as far as curriculum is concerned. Two examinations (the General Certificate of Education at Ordinary Level, and the Certificate of Secondary Education) still exist for the sixteen year old. The former has in the minds of some people a superiority or a greater validity which is denied to CSE – largely perhaps because the latter is a regional examination which may be thought (wrongly) to lack the probity or authority of examinations which have national coverage. Secondly, there is still only one examination which can be taken in schools after the age of sixteen: GCE Advanced Level presents the Schools Council for the Curriculum and Examinations (as the successor to the Secondary Schools Examination Council) with problems about unnecessary specialisation, about rigidity and inability to cater for the needs of the non-traditional sixth former very much along lines on which the Higher School Certificate gave difficulty to the Norwood Committee. The curriculum of the secondary school continues to be under constraint.

Are examinations and curriculum inseparable?

How significant examinations are in the shaping of curriculum depends, of course, upon the definition of curriculum which you happen to uphold at any one time. If you talk about a curriculum as being marketable or as providing the pupil with profitable skills, the need for testing and labelling through some system of examinations is essential. If you talk of curriculum as being that which reveals separately to each pupil some particular significance in this or that aspect of learning, then examinations will not matter much; it will be sufficient that the curriculum is a process of learning in itself.

But if a middle course leads us to accept that some examination, at some level and at some time or another in the pupil's school career is unavoidable, then the questions to be asked about the effect of examinations on curriculum must be posed in another way. Can examinations truly reflect the pupil's attainment at any one instant of time? Can they simply record achievement without measuring it? If examinations are seemingly bound to measure achievement, is there any way of avoiding the need to make examinations a method of stretching the pupil? Are examinations, in other words, separable from the setting of standards? The short answer seems to be no, they are not.

This can be expressed in another way; the major consideration is the relationship between curriculum and examination. The relationship will be most exact when examinations duplicate, as nearly as may be, the recent school work of candidates. It will be least exact when some questions or tasks are passed which the ablest pupils can perform almost without thinking (since the relevant knowledge has long become part of their basic stock-in-trade) and other problems are set which require knowledge well beyond the reach of the weakest candidates. In practice the relationship can never be exact. The gradual shading of levels of ability within the schools, variations in curricular and organisational patterns both within and between schools, differences between subjects, variations in the quality of the teaching and consequently in the pupils' response to exposure to a given area of knowledge (and deficiencies in examining techniques), all these are amongst the factors which make it impracticable to secure an exact match between curriculum and examination.

A description like this drawn from the Seventh Report of the Secondary Schools Examination Council (1963, *Scope and Standards of the Certificate of Secondary Education*) shows that it is a comparatively recent development that people should worry about the purposes of examinations to the extent of trying to do something about their effects on the child's process of learning. Until the post-war period, concern which was felt about the narrowing of curriculum did not appear (apart from gestures such as those of the Northern Joint Matriculation Board, which have already been noticed) to get anywhere. One reason for ineffectiveness lay in the acceptance of examinations as a necessary process, admittedly unreliable and chancy but still essential.

The unreliability of examinations had for some time been under attack quite separately from the judgements which were being made by the Secondary Schools Examination Council. In 1932, C. W. Valentine carried out a careful study of three aspects of unreliability. This work (*The reliability of examinations: an enquiry*) antedated the classic analysis of Hartog and Rhodes on the unreliability of essay marking and rehearsed arguments about the predictive value of examinations which are still to be heard thirty and forty years later.

Present-day concern with the effect of examinations on curriculum is confined to the secondary school. We have already seen what happened when there was an insistence on group examination for older pupils. But we might easily forget the long term impact which tests made, for many decades, on the curriculum of younger children. In 1931 the *Report of the Consultative Committee on the Primary School* (the second Hadow Report) followed up several critiques of what were known as Free Place examinations for entry into grammar schools. The Board of Education had published a memorandum in 1928 and the Welsh Department of the Board had published another contribution on the same subject in 1930. In the same year the Association of Education Committees and the National Union of Teachers jointly published their report on *Examinations in Public Elementary Schools*. Although the growth of differing types of secondary school, resulting from the 1926 Hadow Report (*The Education of the Adolescent*), was expected to diminish the need to select children for grammar schools by competitive examination, a method of classifying pupils by the results of a qualifying examination would always be needed as long as grammar schools existed.

In the 1970s, grammar schools do still exist; they are marginally fewer in number but many pupils in primary schools still have to sit an eleven plus examination. Just as in 1931, so even now it is possible seriously to ask questions about the ill-effects of tests in arithmetic (or mathematics) and English (or verbal reasoning) on the curriculum of primary schools. Just as forty years ago it was fashionable to point to Free Place examinations as disturbing the balance of children's courses in primary schools, so it can currently be claimed that curriculum is more free in junior schools or junior departments in those areas where secondary education has been reorganised in a comprehensive pattern – and where no eleven plus tests survive.

But even where the tests do survive, teachers can be exhorted that there is no reason for distortion of the curriculum: 'The conception of the primary school and its curriculum must not be falsified or distorted by any form of school test whether external or internal; the technique of examination must accordingly be so developed that it keeps abreast of that steady process of humanising and broadening the course of study in the primary school' (*The Primary School*, 1931).

This was a very pure line of thought. It was (and is) unrealistic since tests had to go through very considerable refinements until, at their last degree of sophistication, they were discredited in the late 1950s and early 1960s. Even then they were discredited not because they failed to do their job but because the system to which they were linked had itself lost public approval. It was indeed said in the UNESCO World Survey of Education in 1961 that 'Great Britain has made the greatest advance ... in developing reliable and valued methods of testing and examining scholastic aptitude and ability. Few countries ... have yet adopted such reliable methods of standardising or normalising the marks in assessments used for selection purposes.'

Nevertheless there was, in a system of perfect or near perfect testing, bound to be coaching and cramming, there was bound to be a concern that a school should do as well as it could – for its own sake as well as for individual children – in the public showing of test results. Even after the abolition of the Free Place system, proof of the superiority of a primary school lay in the number of grammar school places which a primary school's pupils 'won'.

Selective examinations were bound, then, to affect curriculum. Valentine had even gone so far as to worry about the unreliability of tests lest they did not do justice to the teacher: he feared, for instance, that another reason for suspecting the reliability of some examinations as a comparative estimate of the ability of candidates could be that pupils came from different schools in which the standard of teaching might greatly vary. Thus children who had been specially well taught had an advantage. And incidentally, felt Valentine, this fact had an unfortunate repercussion on some schools in areas where the entrance examination was regarded as a test of the work of the elementary schools. This was, he admitted, unfair to those schools who drew their pupils from poorer homes, where not only were the conditions for work less favourable both physically and mentally but the children might 'possibly be of lower inborn mental capacity'.

This revealing remark shows not only some of the views about primary school education which were held in Britain in the early 1930s but also some of the attitudes which survive alongside what remains of the present day's eleven plus. Schools are still assessed by the outside world; children are still under stress. They may be under less stress now than in the past; the Plowden Report commented on this and suggested that growing opportunities offered by GCE courses in secondary modern schools probably explained why parents were complaining less about selection. Allocation to a particular kind of secondary school at the age of eleven was no longer quite so unalterable. The same report went on to examine the allegation that selection procedures still led to a narrowing of primary school curriculum because of an excessive emphasis on the acquisition of measurable skills and rigid streaming. A survey carried out by Her Majesty's Inspectors showed, however, that the ill-effects of selection on curriculum were lessening. The suggested reason for this was that teachers' estimates of a child's potential were tending to replace externally imposed attainment tests. But at the same time it could be said that when enquiries had been made into the quality of primary school work where comprehensive schools had already been set up or where testing had been replaced by teachers' estimates, some teachers, not surprisingly, continued their established routines – even when the reason for them has disappeared. Books of English exercises and of mechanical computation remain in many schools.

More realistically the Welsh equivalent of Plowden, the Gittins Report, saw that even when the selective system of secondary education disappeared, the problems of classification, allocation and guidance of children could not be abolished: these would continue to exist in a different context. 'Indeed, as selective examinations and tests at the age of transfer are abolished, there is a considerable danger that they will reappear early in the secondary school. The procedures ... are likely to be less reliable and less subject to technical control and public scrutiny.'

This hard-headed statement is proved accurate by the concern of those who teach in comprehensive schools to do something about non-streaming, setting and banding. Selection *within* secondary schools seems to do something organic, subject to rapid development and difficult to control unless specific steps are taken *not* to select. Meanwhile, in primary schools where the eleven plus still exists, Gittins accepted that it took courage and confidence to swim against the stream and to accept the belief that children can follow a broad curriculum, giving scope for experience and activity and yet do well in a selective examination. There was certainly no reason why a selective examination system could not co-exist with a liberal curriculum. 'Nevertheless, because of the attitudes and practices involved, the selective examination has formed a major obstacle in the way of progressive developments in the primary school.'

A new view of assessment

A shift in policies about examinations usually affects what is taught. In understanding how to manage change in the curriculum it is important to know whether the pressure comes from changes in philosophy about assessment or whether the alteration of curriculum has implications for the way in which it may be examined. The latter question is now confined to the secondary school. The first question needs elaboration and an example.

The successive suggestions made by the Schools Council for the reform of post-sixteen examinations have, particularly from some university GCE Boards, met with suspicion and hostility. As a body which is immediately responsible to the Secretary of State for Education and Science for the public examinations policies of England and Wales, the Council has to accept that its solutions are bound to be those which can be contained within a centralised policy; but the changes which it proposes at any time are likely to fit the circumstances of some schools better than others.

What, then, is the Schools Council trying to do? It is attempting to get some element of reliable prediction into sixth form examinations. It is trying to improve the comparable validities of the syllabuses and markings of what are at present separate examining boards. It is also trying – and this is the principal goal of its efforts – to help along the process of improving sixth form curriculum.

In this attempt the Council starts with the disadvantage that narrowness and excessively early specialisation have been attributed as the evils of an examination system for a very long time. It is not clear what the benefits of a greater breadth of curricular choice would actually be, nor is it clear either that all pupils who are affected are likely to benefit equally from a deferring of the moment of specialisation or that all schools could, apart from the requirements of examinations, *allow* specialisation to be deferred. Some schools need to impose early specialisation in order to get the best out of their limitations of staff, subject departments or buildings. Examination choices can, after all, be affected by a school's organisation in total independence of national policy and of any pupil's exercise of will.

However, because the sixth form examination system is under scrutiny its curriculum, too, is the subject of an organised review. Because minority time, general studies and the continued general education of older pupils are issues which are inseparable from those of examination reform, it is not surprising that curriculum development projects are under way which are intended to respond to these other reforms. The fact that, for instance, the University of York's Sixth Form General Studies project has moved further and faster than actual changes in examinations, matters little. What does matter is that curriculum development at the level of national projects can stem from proposed changes in methods of examining. And this can work downward through the age-groups, too; thus, for instance, general studies in the sixth form are seen as being somehow linked with the systematic reform of studies in the humanities of the fourth and fifth years. On this is based much of the work of the Humanities Curriculum Project at the University of East Anglia.

It is encouraging that changes in what is taught as well as in teaching method can be triggered off by examination reform. This must be far more heartening than having, over the years, to listen to continuous complaint (and no action) about the sterility of examinations. And indeed this is a sure benefit of the joint responsibilities of the Schools Council – responsibilities both for examinations *and* for curriculum.

But it is claimed that change in curriculum has in the past been stifled by the examination system. When, therefore, reform such as that of the Humanities Curriculum Project requires that pupils should work very plainly across subject boundaries, and that they should in every way be encouraged to see the interrelationship of learning which might otherwise fall under the separate titles of history, geography, religious education or social studies as one thing rather than many, it would be nonsensical to require that these should be separated again solely in order that pupils should be capable of gaining a greater number of examination credits. Despite this the Certificate of Secondary Education has in only one or two parts of the country been the subject of experiment in cross-disciplinary examining.

Nevertheless CSE is open to novelty despite the slow response to the opportunities for new freedom provided by Mode III (papers internally set and marked, to the school's own syllabus, but with external moderation of the marking). The irony about the efforts which are now being made to find the best way to give examinable worth to work done in the Humanities Curriculum Project is likely to be that the teachers, their methods of teaching, the examining boards, the Schools Council – that all these will be amenable to the changes which are needed but that the stumbling block will be the desire of pupils to have several separate labels of success (in history, geography, social studies, etc.) rather than one – and simply because it will look better on a certificate. It can only be hoped that those who persist in their attempts to make new curriculum in the humanities acceptable, worthwhile and realistic are strong enough to defeat the wish of pupils – or (as is far more likely) of their parents – to continue to have traditional rewards for non-traditional work. Or are the wishes of pupils and parents indomitably strong? And indeed should the wishes of pupils and their parents be indomitable?

Summary

The answer to any question about the influence of examinations on curriculum – and how much – must in the end be factual rather than a matter of hypothesis. The effect of examinations has been so far unavoidable because the expectations of many people and institutions – schools, parents, employers, the universities and professions, the world of technical education – have led curriculum in the secondary school to be something which fits the process of assessment rather than the other way round.

However, beyond the clearly marked effects of examinations, there are less easily defined but positive influences on curriculum which have their sources outside schools; these include those who act as critics or influences, the writers of textbooks, official publications, advisers and inspectors. The first two categories mainly affect curriculum in the secondary school; the latter two also carry weight in the primary school. Indeed, it is in the primary school that suggestion, advice, the exhortation to try another and better way of doing things has the principal effect. Eleven plus tests influence the curriculum of junior classes (8 years to 11 years) less and less each year. They do not appear to affect infant classes (5 to 7 or 8 years) at all.

But if a teacher has what seems to be genuine freedom to choose a curriculum which suits his or her pupils, the manager of curriculum development has to take account of the fact that at some point the outside world will want to know the usefulness of each choice. It is necessary to realise the price which we pay to the concept of accountability by public examination. The manager of change has to decide whether the price is a high one. But he has also to weigh up the other influences which help us to find an answer to the question of who shapes the curriculum. The more accurate our answer to that question, the better can management hope to become.

4 Other forces in the curriculum

Earlier chapters have looked at the history of comparatively simple definitions of curriculum and the purposes of schooling. It has also been possible to look at the genesis of those curricular demands which have been made upon the teacher, at the ways in which he has reacted, at the people who have tried to influence him, at the way in which he has accepted or rejected the advice of others, and at the way in which gradually we have come to accept the curriculum as something which is devised not for the satisfaction of adults but to meet the needs of the children.

To admit this much, early on, is, of course, to betray a belief that it is the child rather than the grown-up who matters more at the centre of education. To adopt this position has a certain naïveté about it; it is a position in which the educator is exposed to misunderstanding and to purposeful disbelief from those who, within other parts of our society, lack credence in the educative process. Neither side is right – totally. The man who wants to make money, the man who wants his employees to have very simple, straightforward skills upon which he can build or which alternatively he can develop in such a way as to make them more marketable – this man has the forces of the market on his side; and the values of the market have a great deal to justify them.

The educator on the other hand is not supposed to have total faith in the values of the market place. He is someone who is detached, somewhat abstract, somewhat idealistic. The educator does not realise that employers and those in industry who can take the young school leaver on to the payroll are making what is in effect a contribution or gift to society. Education certainly does not prepare young people to enter the world of work; education, in terms of compulsory schooling, does not make young adults who are readily willing to accept the norms of another world.

Does education allow those who are within its charge to see that life is not made up of black and white? Varying shades of grey – whether they relate to moral choices or to personal choices or to matters which affect the personal and family economics of each working man – it is these that lie at the heart of education. For those who are interested in curriculum and for those who are interested in the management of curriculum development, the puzzle is to decide whether matters which are as refined, as subtle, as human and as spiritually confusing as these, can properly be dealt with within the curriculum. On the face of it curriculum, curriculum growth, projects, dissemination packs, training courses – all the paraphernalia of official curriculum development makes it appear as if the understanding of personal predilection, of personal whim, difficulty, and of straightforward human waywardness will escape anything that is attempted at school.

Do different pressures create different curricula?

The oversimplifications of the preceding section are inevitable if we are to try to find out whether the curriculum is truly something which is devised or whether it is something which grows naturally, organically and without too much sense of system. We also have to accept simplifications about the objectives of education if we are to be sure in our mind whether curriculum is something where people have clear purposes or where people are simply reacting against each other – or whether people are simply crying out for help when they have little sense of the direction in which they should lead either themselves or those whom they teach.

The people who lie at the source of curriculum have differing motives and different positions from which to work. Some are interested in the development of curriculum in order simply to do good, to improve a system of education which is in their eyes wrong or misdirected or old-fashioned. Others again see curriculum as a field in which they may deliver messages which they have previously been unable to utter. They may see the world in terms in which they have been incapable of interpreting it to others. They may find that the new language of curriculum development gives them both a vocabulary and a new range of purposes which may make their message more significant. Thirdly, there are those who, in the same way as is bound to happen on the fringe of any public activity, see a way of making money, the writers of textbooks, or work books, of work cards, and of the sundry materials with which children learn, the publishers and the makers of apparatus, and the people who enable teachers to teach rather than simply to be preoccupied with creating materials with which their children might learn – all these people, too, have an interest in curriculum development. Curriculum development entails after all a degree of novelty; novelty means new markets; new markets usually mean bigger margins.

The person who manages curriculum development has, therefore, to know not only the needs which lie behind those who want to see curriculum being changed; he also has to see the motives of those who wish to bring the change about. He has to pick his way carefully between those who are fired by altruism, those who are visionaries and those who see education as business.

In themselves none of these three categories need be either exclusive each of the other nor derogatory about the work of the other two. Nevertheless, the manager of curriculum development, whether at national or at local level, has to determine some degree of priority in the attention which is given to the activities of differing categories of worker. He must also realise that there are differing interpretations which the teacher or the person who provides the funds for education or the person who sees the output of education will attach to the overall idea of development.

Curriculum development if it is to be successful in its best sense has to be reputable and well-founded. The manager of change cannot afford to be naïve; he cannot afford to be ignorant nor to be deluded by those who might see some profit in deluding him. In particular he must make sure that those for whom he works, those whom he guides, and those for whom he manages change are themselves made sensitive to the varying levels of persuasion, influence, purpose and validity of the work which they undertake. This chapter will be concerned with those forces which shape curriculum but which are to some extent more marginal than purely official influences.

Publications: the textbook

The fact that a textbook will be, in places, wrong or mistaken or unattractive differs in its significance according to its subject. Some teachers will insist that their subjects (the sciences, history, geography particularly) make textbooks essential. These are the subjects where it is more economical of the teacher's time for the narrative background of a subject to be covered in some way other than by teaching. If it is more economical (and beneficially so), this is because books are used by a teacher who will be able to make good use of the time which is saved. Other subjects (such as aspects of modern languages and mathematics) need textbooks because they are better exemplifiers than even the most inventive teacher. The subjects where instruction has, in part, to depend on learning through drill and by rote are ones in which the example-filled textbook saves time: but, equally, this only carries benefit for the learner if the teacher makes good use of the teaching time and of the teaching energy which has been saved.

Neither of these two relatively easy-to-define uses of a textbook has much to do directly with curriculum. Their indirect effect is simply the release of a teacher's time for some more rewarding task. But what might such a task be? If we are to believe those who advocate tailor-made and individualised learning materials, any spare time should be used by the teacher to create such materials. But to embark on and to continue work of this type is back-breaking. The repetition of effort, the demands on inventiveness, the continual need for a teacher to uncover fresh resources from which to feed his own imagination, all these can be depressing and onerous tasks even for the most gifted, dedicated and ingenious teacher. The Nuffield Project on Resources for Learning recognised the possibly self-defeating style of effort for which teacher-produced materials would make a demand: hence came that project's emphasis on 'starters' and on materials-producing centres manned by people other than day-to-day teachers. The conception of a so-called hive of material-production would do much to take the tedium and effort out of the job of creating individualised materials for learning.

If, on the other hand, time saved by the use of textbooks is not to be used by the teacher in a way which has any relevance to the development of curriculum where, first, does this leave the textbook? Secondly, what development work *can* the teacher take on? The answer to the first question should logically be that the textbook is only used when the teacher is not available, during periods of private study or for homework. This answer bases itself on the assumption that it is essential for the teacher to be *doing* something when he has a group of pupils with him; he can do something collective (class-instruction) or he can concentrate on helping to solve the separate problems which individual children have struck during private study. This would be, ideally, a secondary school picture. In primary schools where textbooks other than readers and reference books tend to be used, if at all, only by older pupils of junior age (8–11 years), the giving of individualised guidance and help would at least be *expected* to be the normal use of a teacher's time.

To the second question, of whether teachers can use time which is allegedly saved by the use of textbooks for some larger task of curriculum development, the answer has to be less definite and less optimistic. Because they are neither trained nor expected to do much on their own in curriculum rather than in separated subjects, it is unlikely that teachers can make good use of saved time. One use could admittedly be the working-up of a contribution to a joint inter-school effort which has been initiated at a local teachers' centre. This, however, has a tinge about it of doing out-of-school work in school time. However unreasonable it should be to entertain such scruples, many teachers would nevertheless feel diffident at not using their *own* time to work on a joint project. A second use could be the planning of inter-year and inter-subject schemes of in-school development of the curriculum. This gets much nearer to an ideal which most teachers would regard as a legitimate contribution to their own school's work. But for such use to be made of time released by turning pupils on to textbooks (or on to teaching machines or some other form of self-teaching programme) requires good planning within the school. It needs, on the part of a Head, sympathy and energy and a determination to plan his way around other people's difficulties. It calls from several or all members of the staff for a readiness first to trust that their groups of pupils will actually work on their own and then a readiness to use time saved with their own pupils for the benefit of a school as a whole, and for the benefit of other teachers' children. The attitudes of some Heads and assistant teachers would make it difficult to gain acceptance for such collaborative ideas even within single schools.

Although, therefore, it may be fashionable to denigrate the textbook it nevertheless could, if it were regarded as a piece of learning material which genuinely met individual pupils' needs, release teachers for work in school time on common projects of curriculum development. But one vital question which implies criticism of textbooks is whether any text can genuinely meet the varied needs of differing pupils within one class or group. Unless separate groups have some homogeneity – of attainment, ability, motivation or interest – and unless a school can afford differing and suitable texts for different groups (which would itself often be doubtful) the gain to the pupil in terms of self-instruction could be negligible.

Another question about the quality of textbooks is whether any book can be consistently appropriate to a pupil's needs. Again, the answer has to be that it seems unlikely that a single text can match the pace, grasp, and differing levels of interest which a pupil will exhibit week by week and term by term. This is the base for the more usual kind of criticism of the textbook: the criticism can only be met by the teacher using books not as savers of his own time but as storage-units – some contents of which he can use as against others which he cannot or will not use.

Intrinsically, then, the textbook is neither a self-made ally nor an opponent to curriculum development. But the management of such development within individual schools has to take account of the quality and disadvantages of textbooks – for whatever purpose they are used, as time-savers-cum-programmes or as storage-units from which to supplement a teacher's instruction. Management also has to take account first of the policies of individual members of staff and of the school as a whole about textbooks, and secondly of the internal organisation of the school. How easy, in other words, is it to carry out any joint staff planning of a total curriculum? As an alternative to the idea of a single school's own schemes for planning its work, the use of textbooks as a method of releasing teachers for work which might benefit a locality of schools – through a teachers' centre – seems less likely to succeed in the present-day climate of teaching.

To examine so briefly the effect of textbooks on shaping curriculum cannot hope to produce a very clear picture; but on balance, books seem less important and certainly less harmful than they were said to be at the start of the national movement of curriculum reform in Britain in the mid-1960s. But if textbooks have a comparatively uncertain significance in the shaping of curriculum, a second force – that of in-service training – should be more powerful. It does after all act directly on the teacher, it is generally innovative

– and sometimes educative – and it can without difficulty be expected to be part of some larger strategy of curriculum development. The effect of this force will be examined in a later chapter.

Publications: the official voice

The part played in the shaping of curriculum by publications has so far been briefly scanned only in relation to the textbook. Official publications also have their effect. In Britain these are most potent when they come from the Department of Education and Science. Despite the protestations of teachers and their associations about their freedom to choose between different practices and materials, it has still to be admitted that some of the most valuable surveys of good teaching can come only from a central government department and from the consolidated reports of a corps of over four hundred inspectors.

The task of surveying the school scene has two aspects. When the Schools Council does it, as in *Enquiry 1*, or in the Sixth Form Surveys which were published in 1970 and 1971, it commissions Government Social Survey to carry out an impartial examination of attitudes, practices, preferences, fears and hopes. The published results are useful, somewhat undervalued (perhaps because their dispassionate statement of one type of truth is disturbing) and very comprehensive: whole domains are under review. When, on the other hand, the Department of Education and Science publishes its pamphlets, these are personal documents. The authors, admittedly, are not identified but behind each statement it is possible to sense a personal valuation. The judgements expressed are not bizarre but nor are they neutral to the point of being vapidly safe.

The usefulness of pamphlets which are based on the distillation of observation on the part of individual inspectors shows in three examples. In 1967 a small publication on the use of school libraries (*The School Library*, DES Education Pamphlet, No. 21) had a marked effect. First, it gave significance to the often unrecognised work of the School Library Association, an energetic and well-intentioned national body, active in its local branches but faced with the usual difficulties of pleading a special case against other priorities for the ways in which money is spent on schools. Secondly, the publication drew attention to deficiencies, drawbacks and lethargies which then surrounded the ways in which some schools handled their libraries. Thirdly, it introduced the beginnings of a new language in which to talk about libraries. The borrowed phraseology of resources, resource centres and so on is, by now, familiar. But it takes time for a new understanding to grow about any part of education. The resources on which depend curriculum, change in curriculum, and the development of new ideas

– these resources have much to do with verbal and pictorial materials. Many areas of new thinking on, particularly, the arts side of the curriculum would be difficult to explore unless changes in the use of traditional libraries were also under way. To get such an airing for novel ideas was one task for an official pamphlet.

A second, equally ephemeral publication underlined much the same type of moral: when, in 1970, the DES published its *Pamphlet 56* on commercial studies it made the first official utterance for a number of years about a field of secondary school work which had become confused. Confusion about the purposes of commercial courses in secondary schools had stemmed partly from the desire to retain pupils beyond the minimum leaving age in courses which would be thought to equip them – particularly girls – for a vocation. Others who were acting on a mistaken policy – as it now seems to be – competed with technical colleges for the retention of young people in full-time continued education, but in schools rather than under the aegis of Further Education. Other schools again were trying to do their confused best according to the tenets of the Newsom Report: they were trying to give their pupils a sense that their school curriculum had a relevance to adult life.

Apart from this not altogether clear-minded trio of policies there may have been some which were even less worthy of commendation. But whatever were the reasons for schools to provide courses in shorthand, typing, commercial mathematics or book-keeping, the overall impression which they gave was one of not doing it very well. It was admitted that more young workers fail because they cannot speak well, spell well, write a coherent sentence, do an accurate computation and behave sensibly and responsibly, than because they have not achieved high speeds in office skills. A main task for the school was conceded to be that of finding ways of encouraging boys and girls to develop their personalities and their general competence to the full. 'We are more likely to succeed if our pupils find enjoyment in a wide variety of academic, aesthetic and practical experience, rather than in secondary courses limited in the main to intensive instruction in narrow skills.' Here was a very straightforward statement about the purposes of education and an equally clear judgement about the competence of schools. It was sufficiently biased and incautious to catch attention and was a useful type of official stricture on at least part of an ailing curriculum.

Rather in the same position as commerce is drama. Here again schools suffer from good work which is ill-understood, from bad work about which there is too much enthusiasm and from a great number of statements about affective education. What is said about the education of the feelings and the education of the whole man risks inflation. National work to bring a closer connection between the arts and the more easily acceptable or useful parts of the secondary school curriculum goes forward only on a limited scale within the Schools Council's programmes. Drama is thought to be unimportant in contrast to certain other subjects and to other problems which surround, for example, the social education of young people.

All the more to be welcomed for these reasons was a straightforward statement from the prime official source. The Department of Education and Science published *Education Survey No. 2: Drama* in 1968. This showed to the Heads of schools and to others who might think that the whole attention of curriculum renewal should be paid to mathematics, English, the sciences and modern languages, that there were other things to worry about. It also showed that drama could assist in certain areas of difficulty within schools where otherwise the arts in general and drama in particular could well have been overlooked. For instance, while no-one would openly deny sympathy with Heads and Principals who are alarmed by the number of subjects that must be covered by a liberal curriculum and by the demands of examination syllabuses, the drama survey suggested that in terms of the full development of a human being the arts of music, dancing, drama, literature, the crafts and the visual arts are as important at one end of the educational spectrum as science and mathematics are at the other. The two worlds were not contradictory but complementary.

A statement of this type had a bias and flavour about it that told the teacher that it was not simply the cautious theorist who paid attention to this part of curriculum. It was the work of people who were committed to a clear task of improving education in the expressive arts. However polite they might be to the sciences, it was their single-mindedness in fostering the arts which was important.

Givers of advice

Official and semi-official publications may have their usefulness – even when they are not explicitly concerned with the task of overall reform of curriculum. They can, of course, be ignored as mere exhortations, unless the Head of a school takes them seriously enough to require some action or unless a local education authority attempts to reshape its policies about, for instance, the appointment of area drama advisers or about the equipping of schools for commercial courses. But given some local concern and some local activity, preferably in the shape of retraining which has been locally organised by a local education authority or through an individual teachers' centre, or by joint university and HM Inspectors' course, then pamphlets and occasional publications *can* have an impact on curriculum development.

But if publications – whether commercial ones or those which emanate from more official sources – are to have an effect, it is important to see that usually something more than the influence of the Head of the school himself is necessary.

The point has been made – and will continue to be made – that the management of curriculum development is different between primary and secondary schools. In the latter the Head is not an expert in curriculum; he is a subject specialist who is in England and Wales untrained either in management of curriculum or in the organisation of his school. He succeeds because he is intelligent, because he is personable, because he has vision, because he has organisational skills – or indeed because he has many other qualities which those who employ him knew nothing about at the time when he was appointed. Because he is not an expert in curriculum management it would be usual to think that he needed help and indeed that he needed help from an outsider.

In primary schools Heads are perhaps more accustomed, by tradition alone, to rely upon advisers, organisers and inspectors to assess the quality of their school, to tell them where to take up points of strength, where to correct points of debility. The interdependence between those in charge of primary schools and those who are in advisory services is something different from the relationship between those in secondary schools and the outside expert.

The difficulty here lies in trying to define what is needed in the management of curriculum development. To those who may regard themselves as the principal managers it would not after all be very unusual if a member of Her Majesty's Inspectorate were to be surprised that we pay so much attention nowadays to this thing called curriculum – as though it had some separate or new identity. The Inspector could well claim that the management of change, the management of improvement, and the management of development has been what he has always been paid to do. The same could be claimed by those who work as advisers or inspectors within local education authorities. It did not, however, need either a select committee of Parliament nor did it need what was known as the Fulton Report to tell those who work in schools and in local authorities that the adviser and the inspector is not a person who has any intrinsic claim to superiority – either of skill or of knowledge in the task of management.

If new ideas are to be put into action, if something is to be attempted which has not been attempted before, if development is to be taken seriously and if it is something which has to be treated systematically, then we have to disentangle the role of the official and quasi-official documentary guidance which floods into our schools from the roles of certain people. Some of these people are HMI and local authority advisers; others are peripatetic tutors of music, or peripatetic remedial teachers – and so on. Their number and their titles are practically legion. Whatever they are called, their influence has to be assessed before we can decide exactly which resources the manager of change has to take seriously.

Depending upon which country you teach in, the outside expert is likely to be called an inspector or a supervisor, or an adviser or a consultant. The subtleties of labelling may be lost on the teacher since in one way or another each outsider is regarded as having some power, some capacity of supervision. The power of the outsider is such that the teacher naturally assumes that someone much higher up thinks that he, the teacher, is in need of oversight.

Admittedly, we tend nowadays not to talk in terms of oversight or supervision but in terms of guidance or support or advice. Because the language is becoming confused and because the role of the outsider in the process of curriculum change is significant either in stimulating or in stopping worthwhile things, it is necessary to try to define the nature of what will simply be called 'supervision'. The one time supervisor has become by now the teacher's friend: is this true? Or is it more true that the outsider, the supervisor, nowadays has a more direct participation in the control, management and improvement of education than he had in the past?

The descriptions about those who help teachers tend to fall into one of two categories. If you are an inspector or an organiser of what a teacher does, this implies some renunciation of the teacher's autonomy. It means that the teacher (because he or she is inspected) is at risk of being thought incapable of coping. It may be that somebody else will have to take over or organise something for us. If, on the other hand, we talk not of inspection and of organising but of advice and consultation, then the autonomy of the teacher is preserved. If I ask for advice, it is because I think that I *might* be able to do things better than I at present manage them. Even so, I wish first to be the judge of whether an alternative way of doing things is better than my present way of operating. Comparably if I ask for a consultant, then in anything other than crises of ill-health or bankruptcy or of industrial disaster, I may reject the advice which the consultant gives me. It may be that my only chance of survival would be to work on the advice that he has chosen to give me; nevertheless as a teacher I do have some professional right to refuse to survive.

The language of professional survival is, of course, rather extreme; a teacher can fall well short of any attempt to improve or to develop curriculum without being in professional jeopardy. There are no statutory standards by which to measure the efficiency of teaching in England and Wales.

We speak very mutedly about control and influence and on the whole it seems to work best if we do not acknowledge that the teacher is free to teach only in the sense that he is free to choose upon whom or what to be dependent. If he is dependent upon poor textbooks or upon a badly remembered experience of his own time in school, if he chooses to be dependent upon cynical advice of friends or upon the bad advice of journals and journalists, if he chooses to be dependent upon nothing more than an ill-considered whim – practically nothing can be done to change or to improve a teacher. It may be that he needs practical help, it may be that he would welcome specific aid if it were offered to him in the right way by the right person. The point is that the manager of curriculum development has very little knowledge of who it is who would best help a particular teacher. The manager likewise has very little sense of the particular kind of assistance which an individual teacher can be given at one moment.

There seems to be only one thing about which we can have certainty: if a teacher needs help, the help that he will welcome will be that of someone who works alongside him with the children, with the particular problem of this classroom and of this learning group. The teacher will not welcome gratuitous advice nor will he welcome exhortation which is vague and unpointed. It does not matter how friendly the inspector or the supervisor or the adviser can be. What matters is that when the teacher needs help in the shape of an expert or an experienced or specially skilled person who knows more than he does, then that person should be there to give him what he needs. Distance, abstractness, vague influence – these are not what are wanted. Teachers welcome specific aid – how to organise a room, how to secure the right equipment, what to read, how to try to influence another teacher, how to influence his own Head. These are matters which belong to the practical world and they have a further dimension to add to those influences which are brought to bear upon the development of the curriculum.

It is perhaps because they were in the past given too much advice which they did not want that members of the teaching profession in England and Wales believe that they have to be free of burdensome supervision. The reason for this wish for freedom is not often stated in specific form; a result is that the significance of inspection, advice and supervision has been gradually whittled down. In the 1922 Report on Education it was stressed that 'no feeling of antagonism need be or is generally engendered' by the respective functions of teachers and inspectors. Would inspectors and advisers become, in the words of a later Senior Chief Inspector, Sir Percy Wilson, nationally and locally 'superfluous and derogatory' if teachers were better organised to plan their own curriculum?

But if teachers are indeed organised to attend to their own professional standards, there would probably have been little or no concern in the 1960s to alter or to improve curriculum. In one way, Britain's interest in reform at that time followed the by now well-known pattern of a concern which was first expressed by a minority, then shared with a larger number of educators and public figures, and finally made the subject of legislation and of liberal financial programmes. This, we are told, was the pattern in the United States in the late 1950s and afterwards. The most popular explanation of why this should have happened in that country is that of claiming educational reform to be a direct consequence of the implications – for defence, for the national economy and ultimately for national prestige – of the Soviet space programme. In 1957-8 the launching of Sputnik and consequent reproaches about an educational system which could not produce technologists who could compete with the Russians – these, we are told, had a powerful effect on Federal policies. Models of reform in the teaching of science and mathematics were quickly built up.

These had their impact on England and Wales on the work of the Nuffield Foundation in similar fields. Gradually the ripples of effect moved outward.

Summary

Official edicts, the philosophies of educational visionaries, people, books, tradition and history, each of these has made an impact on the curriculum of schools in England and Wales. The attempt has been made in this part of the book to show that curriculum development is an untidy part of the English educational scene. The way in which curriculum development has worked and works at present is the result of a mixture of forces – some intentioned, some quite unintentional – which have acted more or less for the benefit of the nation's children. The second half of the book will attempt to show how the comparatively amorphous tradition which we have inherited might be put into better shape within the next twenty or thirty years.

No one would seriously think that the management of curriculum change in a country with a comparatively long tradition of democratic education could be made into a matter of models or prescriptions or of neat definition. The teacher in England and Wales is fortunate today in that he has taken over a culture of teaching from the minds and practices of men of considerable conscience, skill, authority and wisdom in the past. Curriculum, and the development of curriculum, has been part of the fabric of English education from at least the early years of the twentieth century.

It would be presumptuous to claim that the management of curriculum change is something very new or scientific or mystical. If, on the other hand, we went too far the other way, if we were to be too pragmatic, if we were to claim that – in common with so many good English activities – everything would come out best if we depended upon goodwill and commonsense, the risk would be that we would betray future generations of children.

The development of curriculum has to be something to which a certain

SUMMARY

amount of rigorous thought has to be paid. It has to be rigorous in order to be honest but it need not be rigorous in order simply to be logical. It could be argued that curriculum need not be too tightly structured; more realistically it could be argued that the structure of curriculum should be one which is organic rather than logical, something of a comparatively loose creative fit rather than with a tight cognitive pattern.

The next part of this book will describe attempts which have been made to systematise the development of curriculum, to draw attention to some of the weaknesses of such systems as now operate, to draw distinctions between national and local efforts, and to point a few morals about the way in which the pace and the quality of change in education might be reflected in the future of curriculum development.

PART TWO

Truisms

Truisms can be skipped; if they are actually read, the reader may so easily agree with what is said that he will pass with greater rapidity to the next stage of the argument. If he disagrees, he may be irritated to the point of wondering why any idea at all is assumed to be shared. The natural reaction then will be that he will reject what is to be said next or (and this is far more likely) have far better ideas for himself.

The curriculum of a school is something which is often passively tolerated, by teachers and by pupils alike. There can be uncertainty about the amount of room for manoeuvre, about how much can be challenged, or replaced, or rebuilt.

The individual teacher will not readily expect that he himself has a very active role to play in developing or in changing things. He will not regard himself as an user of curriculum; rather, he will expect to be the agent who is used in order to transmit to, or share with, his pupils certain quite specific pieces of knowledge, experience or insight. It should not be surprising if the individual teacher does not see his own work as being particularly relevant to the seemingly much larger entity which we call curriculum. But if the management of curriculum reform is to be successful, we could reasonably expect that it should create at least some sense of that over-used idea of relevance.

Relevance has been described as being the connection between what you know and your movement towards goals you care about. To do something about what you care for implies some power to act; to have such a power necessitates that you convert a body of knowledge into what jargon sometimes describes as 'generative rules' – that is, ways of thinking about the world and about yourself. J. S. Bruner said this in a lecture in 1970; about fifty years earlier E. M. Forster had laid a comparable guilt on the world – 'Only connect'. But if in education we feel that we are not assisted in the task of equipping ourselves with what the socio-psychologists describe as effective convictions, it may partly be the fault of the machine with which we work. If we use traditional methods in order to achieve an allegedly (but probably illusory) new aim of redesigning curriculum, then we need to know the condition of the machine; will it stand up to a new task?

The answer is that a strong system of public education will tolerate almost any strain. Historians of education carefully remind us about the struggles which once concerned confessional education. Those who created the context within which we can today dispassionately discuss secular curriculum had to enter into arguments in which their commitment to particular beliefs stood revealed to a number of interpretations. No doubt in their time they disliked the coarsening and oversimplifying of their value-positions in much the same way as we would today: but unless they had been prepared to tolerate such a coarsening we would not by now have moved so far towards our easily accepted sophistication of educational argument.

That we should refuse to be continually neutral and that we should show clearly what we care for – this is one plea: a second plea is that education should concentrate more on what is unknown and speculative than on what is known and established. When we talk of curriculum this brings into conflict two sets of teachers, those whom we all recognise as knowers and those who, with more humility, are seen as active seekers. The knowers look at ideas, stimulating or not, with which any external agency provides them; they see new concepts as forming a framework *within* which to work. The seekers on the other hand are those who see 'given' philosophy as a fresh goad; they prefer some invitation to speculate and to doubt rather than to accept other people's declarations.

To speculate and to doubt implies, of course, that there is something on which actually to cast doubt. Certainly most activity connected with curriculum is open to second thoughts; equally certainly the easiest things to destroy through doubt are ideas. But ideas are free and plentiful. What is harder to find is invulnerable practice, practice which stands up to criticism. This is partly J. J. Schwab's argument (*The practical, a language for curriculum*) when he says that the core around which curriculum *theory* is built is made up of abstract or idealised representations of reality, while curriculum in action treats with real things, real acts, real teachers, real children – richer than (and different from) their theoretical representations.

To cast doubt on theory is, by this argument, a simple exercise if only because theories anyway – and almost invariably – fall short of comprehending the whole of what they try to explain. To reveal inadequacies of action, on the other hand, usually means that frictions and failures in the machinery have to be identified and put right. If, too, the practical outcome of a curriculum is examined, this will show up its shortcomings and inadequacies; the kind of doubt which is produced by an awareness of practical failure will be likely to lead to a more useful type of speculation about improving future ways of doing things.

The variety of futures for which a curriculum can prepare the learner is, in theory, unlimited. The alternatives are plentiful: you can dream up a future by various methods, each with its own jargon. You can extrapolate a trend, you can use what are called Delphi techniques (that is, ask a number of people what they think should happen in the future and, as exactly as they can suppose, when it should happen, collate their answers and forecast a certain type of future). Or you can use what is called normative forecasting (that is, decide what you want to happen and work backward through the necessary steps until you reach the position where you now are). Or you can use straight and fundamental research. Each of these methods of planning lies by definition in the realm of theory and speculation – without there being any necessary relevance for the practical domain of how things actually work.

5 Current English systems of curriculum development: the national picture

There are two difficulties about describing national systems of reform. The first is that whoever it is who admits the description is accurate is bound to have either an outdated view or a view that is lopsided. Alternatively, he is likely to be committed to the idea of national reform or to be somewhat cynical about the effects of national renewal.

If one looks back into the history of educational reform in England and Wales, two names immediately come to mind. Both belong to men who were eminent in Her Majesty's Inspectorate, Matthew Arnold and Michael Sadler, who were each responsible for looking at the systems of education which prevailed in the late nineteenth and the early twentieth centuries in other countries. Because they were men who knew how to play their cards, they chose, instead of saying that the British way of doing things was somehow wrong, simply to point to how things were being done elsewhere.

The technique of showing that people in other countries do things differently from the ways in which we do things ourselves is fairly persuasive. It contains the fallacy, of course, that because it is being done well in another country something can be done equally well here. The jargon no doubt calls this the fallacy of cultural transference. By this point in the twentieth century, however, there are few people who are so unsophisticated as to expect that that which works in the United States of America or in the Soviet Union or in Australasia can be applied directly or even after modification and amendment to Britain. More especially, the problems which apply to the transference of ideas of public service from one country to another preoccupy those whose responsibility it is to look after the spending of money in developing societies – particularly in the Third World.

Education is a sophisticated activity; when in the late 1950s and early 1960s a certain British Minister of Education found a new interest in European methods of education he was too wise to assume that the lessons he learned elsewhere could be applied to his own system. Because of this he (equally wisely) turned the problem over to his professionals. The most that could be done at a time when people felt some unease about the quality of English education was that someone should be concerned about it, that he should try to involve one or two other people in worrying about it, and that a number of people in the end might come up with some type of solution which would be likely to persuade and to inspire the majority of those who are involved in the process of education in England and in Wales.

Even to say this is, of course, to admit that within the English way of doing things, system matters much less than the person. If anything was wrong with English education it was not something that could be put right by having a highly philosophical, Gallic-type 'polytechnicien' line of approach. If there was to be reform in English education, if there was to be some redesign of the curriculum, if there was to be some appeal that the teacher should accept responsibility for quality in the purpose of what he taught, then the approach would have to be very different from that which had been adopted in other countries.

Because it was people rather than systems which mattered, it is not unnatural that the myth which has grown around men like Derek Morrell should become part of the current history of curriculum development in this country.

The first attempt at a national renewal of curriculum was centred on a body known as the Curriculum Study Group; the CSG was set up early in 1962 and consisted of some members of Her Majesty's Inspectorate and one or two others. Because they belonged to central government they immediately attracted the wrath of the teacher associations. In that respect it is easy to see that the attempt to create some inner cabinet for the reform of education was misjudged. With customary agility and with a quick sense not only of diplomacy but of the necessities of education, men like Morrell, together with their ministers, suggested and launched a Working Party. The Working Party produced its report in the briefest time in which any committee might promulgate its proposal. With very rapid agreement from the teacher associations and from local authority associations it was possible in 1965 for the Schools Council for Curriculum and Examinations to be set up. Its early history has been well-documented and its early working papers are well known. It had succeeded the Secondary Schools Examination Council, but it had, of course, expanded its brief so as to include matters of curriculum affecting children fom the age of two to the age of eighteen.

The way in which this central body was funded (to the extent of about one million and a half pounds a year), the way in which it was supported by all the partners of education, the way in which it set to work with a small devoted secretariat, all this is a credit to Lord Redcliffe-Maud, and, on the executive side, to Derek Morrell. This is not the place to pay tribute to those who have advanced educational causes. Nevertheless, had not the conception of a centralised concern of curriculum renewal been born in the mid-1960s it would have been completely feasible that Britain would have fallen out of the race with other developed countries in maintaining and improving a modern system of education which did credit not only to its own people but also to the overall conception that educators might be the people to improve the quality of life.

National plan and process

When we look more closely at the workings of the Schools Council in its early years we are bound to be struck first by the largeness of its ambitions, and secondly, by the naïveté of its hopes.

For instance, the first three working papers were devoted respectively to providing a new approach to science teaching for unwilling learners in secondary schools, secondly to providing some form of new curriculum for those who were to be affected by the raising of the minimum school leaving age to sixteen in 1972, and thirdly to improving the overall teaching of English both in primary and in secondary education. These first three working papers are good examples to analyse in some detail.

In 1972 the Schools Council had about 120 projects at work. Of these about twenty involved examinations, five were to do with specifically Welsh problems, another five were to do with the organisation of schools and their resources, and another half dozen or so dealt with school, home and community. Of the remainder eight were devoted to mathematics and fifteen were devoted to science. This latter batch might be the more interesting to look at in the first place.

The very first working paper of the new Schools Council was given the title of *Science for the Young School Leaver*. The origins of the paper lay in the discontent with science teaching which was felt by senior members of Her Majesty's Inspectorate, by one or two people who taught in schools, in colleges and at universities in the early 1960s. By some curious chemistry (the secrets of which we shall never know) enough people of common mind came together for it to be possible for a plan to be born. The plan was a simple one. The Schools Council existed and the Schools Council had the right to publish working papers. These working papers could not be claimed to have the status of anything more than documents for discussion. If it was necessary – as this small group of devoted people who were concerned with science felt – that science education should improve, then a discussion paper put out by the Schools Council would reach a wide audience, would have the reputable backing of a semi-government institution and might also lead to action.

The drafting of Working Paper No. 1 is something which lay between members of Her Majesty's Inspectorate, one or two gifted specialists in the field of science, and one or two senior Civil Servants. What the paper said was a reflection in some detail of what had been said in the Newsom Report (*Half Our Future*) in 1963. Those who attend secondary schools in England and Wales do so somewhat unwillingly unless they see a purpose in their attendance. They see such a purpose in attending school if they are likely to pass examinations or if the subject which they learn is likely to be useful to them later in life. The first working paper specifically set out to look at science in a new way – first, so as to prove more interesting and secondly, so as to prove more, as the jargon of the Newsom Report had by then led us to accept, relevant to life. The paper suggested that science embraced many matters which concern the economics of life together with matters of both moral and political importance. Ideas were outlined which suggested that science might have something to do with education as a whole and that it should not be simply compartmentalised as one subject. In one way, the working paper did very little other than to reproduce in a new form ideas about thematic teaching which had been current in the 1920s and in the 1930s. What was important about the first working paper of the Schools Council, however, was that the message was delivered with urgency, with plausibility, and with a sense that something could be done.

What was done took two forms. First, the Schools Council made more firm a commitment which it had already made jointly with the Nuffield Foundation for the support and dissemination of a certain number of science projects for young children and for older pupils. These projects, which are mainly known as Nuffield Science, are complicated and ramify widely over fields of science in both specialised and non-specialised ways. The history of the Nuffield Foundation's own contribution to curriculum development needs acknowledgement. At this stage, however, it is sufficient to say that *Working Paper No. 1* already had some base of acceptance in schools. Teachers had heard about Nuffield Science, they had realised that money was already being spent – even if it was not public money – on the attempt to renew science teaching. Somewhat surprisingly teachers had been asked to accept that children from the age of five years and eight years could adopt a new approach to thinking about scientific affairs. They had also been given at the level of sixth form teaching and at the level which immediately precedes university entrance in England and Wales, direct assistance in the teaching of physics, chemistry and biology (as well as a combination of the three) which was new, engaging, and, to the skilful science teacher, challenging.

The Schools Council's Working Paper was directed at a different audience. Those who taught science in many of the secondary modern schools of England and Wales were not trained as science specialists. Also, it had been accepted that what Newsom said about the boredom of children in secondary schools was true. Between 1963 and the present day the language has changed. Instead of boredom we talk about reluctance, but the reluctant learner needs as much stimulus and interest to re-engage his capacity to learn as does the child who, in the 1960s, was thought simply not to find education relevant to life.

What the Schools Council had to do was to find someone who could imaginatively and with considerable practical capacity create a development project around the ideas which had been born in the first Working Paper. This person had to find people with like minds to her own, she had to find people in turn who had energy as well as a clear grasp of what was needed. The Schools Council had to supply the money, administrative and other support and, more important than anything else, perhaps, had to make sure that whatever was done by the first project team was given good publicity, was given a wide distribution through acceptable channels of educational publishing, and was given every chance of being understood through a chain of courses of in-service training for teachers.

The third Schools Council working paper was also concerned with part of the field of subjects (this time English) but it differed from the first. Very little was known about the methods of English teaching and equally little was known about the effectiveness of such teaching. It was accepted that English was something which had to be taught in all our schools, that there was a widespread and uneasy certainty that English was not well taught. It was accepted as a necessity because employers asked for it, parents expected it to be taught, and every teacher, as the cant phrase put it, was a teacher of English.

What the third working paper did was to reveal the considerable gaps in our knowledge about the teaching of a particular subject. Very little was known about the purposes of teaching literature, very little was known about the comparatively new concept of oracy, very little was known about the ways in which children acquired language and about the question of whether this connected with the thing that was called English as it was taught in schools. In effect the picture painted by the third working paper was dismal and was compared to a crocheted teacloth; there were many holes.

Unlike the problem of improving the teaching of science, the improvement of the teaching of English had an effect which was far wider. As a subject to be taught, English affected primary schools as well as secondary schools. For the youngest of our pupils, English was difficult to separate from reading – and the teaching of reading has about it a particular mystique which is not present in other parts of the curriculum.

Not surprisingly, the projects which stemmed from the publication of *Working Paper No. 3* were wider in their variety than those which affected the first paper about science. Although there are, still, more national science projects for curriculum development than there are for the learning of English, four of the former are rather small-scale research enquiries into topics such as measuring changes of attitude towards science, two are related specifically towards technology and engineering science and, of the remainder, six are Nuffield-based (i.e. they go back to the first important connection between the Schools Council and the Nuffield Foundation). There are four of what we might call 'new' (i.e. not Nuffield-originated) projects and one is to do with the supply of biological specimens.

By contrast, the English programme includes one project which is directed at pre-school reading skills, one at language development in the primary school, and two at English for immigrant and foreign children.

Of the research projects, one has been concerned with evaluating the Initial Teaching Alphabet; others, however, have ranged from trying to find out what are children's present reading habits (and how significant these may be), to the methods by which children question and respond to questioning at school, to the writing of English (two projects), to oracy, to the effects of linguistics on English teaching and to those larger questions which are posed when we consider children not simply as receivers of English teaching but as readers in their own right.

The difficulties which faced the Schools Council in launching its English programme were complicated. English was, after all, a depressed subject; it was necessary for us to know more about its weaknesses and potentialities. It was also necessary to find people who could catch on to the idea of curriculum change in general and, in particular, of curriculum development in English itself.

Unlike its attempts in the field of science, the Schools Council lacked the inheritance of a network of people, money and influence in trying to reform English teaching. In common with science, however, which had its active Association for Science Education, English teaching, too, is supported by a powerful subject-association (National Association for the Teaching of English, NATE). NATE was to become one of the School Council's best allies – finding ways of filling gaps of knowledge, throwing up the two or three vital leader-figures upon whom development work will always call and, in particular, fostering an understanding of the Council's purposes – and in terms not of English alone but of education as a whole.

The mechanics of central development are deceptively simple: identify a problem, convince a significant forum of the teaching profession that the problem is serious, and find agreement (from amongst those who have money) to finance a research or development programme. Then find someone who is capable of taking on a project, leading a team, working hard and, in a matter of three, four, or five years producing workable answers to major problems.

The answers can come in the form of better information (from research), in exhortatory or inspirational literature (guides, work books, outlines), or as straightforward new teaching materials which are honest, good and uncomplicated enough for the teacher to use with little professional, moral or personal hesitation.

This sounds simple enough, of course, for it to be wondered at that this should ever present a new challenge to our educational system. But behind the simplicities lie slightly sinister questions. Are officially blessed teaching materials intrinsically better than those which are produced, year by year, by educational publishers who look, among other things, for profit? Of course not. Is not the idea of an official blessing alien to British education? Well, not really, but those who fought against the Schools Council in the early days feared the imposition of a centrally controlled curriculum.

Hence, official blessings have their own problems: but official blessing, in terms of the School Council's projects, means no more than that successive trials of sample draft materials have been carried out (with yet more official blessing from LEAs and others) in a large number of schools.

Is the same thing true about official research? No. Few teachers are interested in the findings of educational research except when these confirm what commonsense would have told us in the first place. But for research to be officially backed in Britain does not mean that the funding agency has any particular interest in the findings of that research. No developed country has time to tolerate or to commend research which is deliberately distorted. Any unusual potency of knowledge is, after all, significant only in those societies where ignorance is general and where knowledge (or politically oriented intelligence or what is simply educated power) is overvalued. It may be because of this that there is more interest in England, as in other developed countries, in survey than in research. It means that I find more interest (if not more value) in knowing how people look at things rather than in knowing exactly *why* they have such-and-such an opinion.

Research, survey and the filling of knowledge-gaps were some of the jobs which the Schools Council set for itself. Those who are best at research are usually thought to be university men. The acquisition and analysis of fresh knowledge forms a large part of their professional lives. Hence when the working papers were published a dignified scramble followed. Which university and which Institute of Education would be allowed to search for the new knowledge which was needed? To get into the act meant that some (small) prestige would attach to the operation. More importantly, public funds (those of the Schools Council) could be attracted to the educational side of an university's work. Because education is accepted as a low-prestige part of British university life, it finds itself fairly poorly endowed. Access to new funds means much to morale.

Far the most crucial question, however, lay not in securing the approval of teachers' associations, or in paying for a certain amount of university activity but in finding people who were good enough to lead the creative (if this not over-crudely separates research from action) aspects of the Schools Council's programmes.

To enter deeply into curriculum development certainly involves acquiring fresh knowledge. But it also means that someone with considerable gifts of imagination, practicality, honesty, energy and intelligibility to the so-called average teacher has to be in charge of making materials which can be used in the classroom. In England and Wales, as elsewhere, we have no system for finding leaders for work of this kind. We spot winners – if we are lucky. Repute helps a little; status in itself matters not at all.

In contrast with those working papers which dealt with subjects (Numbers 1 and 3), *Working Paper No. 2* presented a more complicated problem; it revealed some of the difficulties about the young school leaver. It had one antecedent (The Newsom Report) which had barely been digested in the interval since its publication in 1963. It had no highly respectable frame of academic reference. Admittedly, ideas about motivation, deprivation and failure were of interest to some psychologists and to a very small number of imaginative educationists – particularly among those with a taste for sociology.

On the whole, however, the educational world regarded the teenager who did not want to learn as an unavoidable evil. The system would keep him in school until he was fifteen and, later, until he was sixteen. No one was quite sure how to look at the social demands which were to be made on education by the reluctant learner. Should he be realistically attracted to resume or to continue an interest in schooling? Or should we (however shamefacedly) admit that losses must, in the end, be cut?

Not surprisingly, *Working Paper No. 2* was the most imaginative of the School Council's early working papers; it took the ideas of the Newsom Report seriously and it intended to take them to the point of action.

No guidelines

If we look at the number of central projects which took their genesis from *Working Paper No. 2,* we will find that they range very widely in the field of the humanities. Eight projects were launched: these included a project which was meant to produce teaching material, pupil material and a report about religious education; a report about social education; materials and a report about integrated studies; teaching material and pupil material in moral education; comparable materials (together with a report) for the humanities themselves; a project which was to end with a report about the preparation of young people for world citizenship; geography for the young school leaver, and geography both for those who would leave school early and those who would continue beyond the minimum leaving age.

In the field which the Schools Council describes as creative studies, three projects relate to the programme for young school leavers. One is intended to result merely in a report about physical education in secondary schools; another is intended to produce teaching materials and a report about arts and the adolescent; and another is meant to give access to both teaching and pupil materials in design and craft education.

Mathematics has one major project related to RSLA (*Mathematics for the Majority*) and this is comparable to the major project within the science programme which was outlined in *Working Paper No. 1* and which led to the design and launching of the *Science for the Young School Leaver* project.

Another category of research and development is described by the Schools Council as falling within the field of 'interrelated studies'. In this area the young school leaver is intended (hopefully) to benefit from an enquiry and report on the effects of mass media on the secondary school, from a project to produce teaching materials on careers education and guidance, on a research report on industriousness and achievement in school, and on a pair of projects which (taking their origins from those who are aged five and which are intended to cover the needs of all those up to the age of sixteen) are concerned with the deficiencies of that type of education which is at present provided for those who learn very slowly.

One project about connections with the school, the home and the community stemmed from the second Working Paper. One report on the connection between youth service and schools was also to yield some significant information about the way in which formal relationships between teachers and pupils (and less formal relationships between youth leaders and members of youth groups) differed, why they differed and how they might supplement each other.

Two projects concerned with school organisation and resources also have a connection with RSLA. The first deals with those factors in school organisation which influence pupil involvement and the second is intended to provide new information about team teaching in integrated studies for pupils at the younger end of the secondary age range.

In contrast with what it had set out to do in the description of its programmes for science and for English, the Schools Council in its discussion paper about the young school leaver indicated possible lines of action where no guidance had previously been offered. There had been exhortation in plenty; now was the time for something rather more firm.

The twenty or so projects which have been briefly outlined reveal how a central agency for curriculum development can set about reform. In an area of learning, motivation, social organisation and school involvement about which little has been known other than in terms of crude practice, the Schools Council has set out to provide information, material and teacher guidance. Yet it is likely that the *total* result of the RSLA projects will still have greater value in terms of exhortation and inspiration than in the realm of active support or practical assistance in the classroom.

What do teachers need?

One of the ironies of a programme which has the novelty of the Schools Council leaving age programme could be that it will provide help of the kind for which teachers deny a need. The majority of members of the Schools Council are serving teachers. More significantly the majority come from the major teaching union, the National Union of Teachers. Teacher unions in every country are known to believe in the capacity of the teacher to determine his own professional future and to define his own professional needs.

In England and Wales, the NUT is not unique in the claims that it makes for preferring practical assistance to knowledge about research. The NUT in common with all practising teachers who believe that their work is a craft rather than a science also has frequently expressed the opinion that examples of good practice are of more value than the production of model teaching materials. No one is particularly anxious to know what mere theoreticians can recommend. And yet it is likely to be the novelty, controversy and stimulation of national projects which matters more than materials or practical guidance.

In comparing the effects of the first three Working Papers of the Schools Council it needs to be remembered that a document which is directed at the science teacher assumes that he is in some way trained in the teaching of science. Comparably, but perhaps with no very real basis in fact, a document which tries to draw the attention of those who teach English assumes that English teachers are trained in or otherwise committed to one subject.

By contrast a programme which makes demands which are as broad as those of RSLA is directed at a variety of what the jargon calls target populations. Those who taught fourth year leavers in secondary schools were sometimes teachers who had failed in other parts of curriculum. Sometimes those who were concerned with early leavers were devoted to a concept of something which we loosely describe as remedial or compensatory education. This concept seems to be ill-understood in England and Wales, and if the British are to draw from the experience of the United States, attempts in compensation at school are unlikely to succeed in making up for deficiencies for which homes are responsible.

Teachers who are involved in projects which stem from *Working Paper No. 2* may be lethargic or devoted to their teaching; they may be general subjects teachers or highly trained specialists; they may be optimistic or fearful about any move to keep children in school beyond the age at which they wish apparently to stay. Each of these factors presents a considerable challenge to the conception of curriculum development which has breadth and imagination.

If curriculum development on a national scale succeeds in any – if not in all – of the twenty projects which are connected with RSLA, something will have been proved about education in England and Wales. We shall have had some new conviction about the way in which teachers in secondary schools are prepared to put away old prejudices and to accept (or if not accept, at least to try) new ideas, new methods, new attitudes.

In a context such as this, *Working Paper No. 2* provided a simple challenge and required a stronger response than most of the demands which had previously been made in the name of curriculum development. Whether or not that response will be forthcoming is something which it will need perhaps half a decade yet to prove. The only point which needs to be made here is that three differing approaches can produce three differing types of strategy and response.

Differences of response to national change

Because teachers themselves vary in their professional expectations, in their experience, and in their attitude towards innovation, the crucial differences between the Schools Council's first three attempts at setting the stage for curriculum development will provide useful but, perhaps, not demoralising information about how to manage reform.

When one looks back from a position of experience at what was being attempted in the late 1960s and the early 1970s, it is likely that national development projects will be found to depend for their success on personalities rather than upon principles, formulae or clearly demarcated programmes. If this is so, it will not be surprising within the typically pragmatic definiton of educational advancement in this country. It may mean that those who pinned their faith on the capacity for American types of reform to be translated into the British system will be disappointed. It may mean that believers in theory will, once more, despair. If national reform fails to fall into a neatly definable pattern, it will disappoint some of those who believe that innovation can be systematic. The ways in which national projects succeed or fail are likely, however, to be less significant than attempts to reproduce a change at a local level.

Analysis of local success and failure must be preceded by a brief examination of the ways in which central reform works. The questions which must be answered about national projects are

- how is a decision made about the subject areas which need reform?
- by whom were these decisions made?
- how is it decided what a decision about reform will entail in terms of resources and of public success and failure?
- how will it be decided which teaching circumstances are likely to be the most favourable and the least favourable for success in the attempt which is made by any new project?
- by whom will it be judged that a project is likely to succeed?
- how will we know if a project fails?

Each of these questions depends upon one larger question which has to be answered – even if it is only a speculative one – before any attempt is made at reform. Unless a good idea can be rendered into good practical shape (usable, credible, practicable and of direct relevance to the teacher) and unless an idea is likely to be successfully diffused, we need not enter into any second phase. New ideas are not likely to be forced on teachers in England and Wales. Centralisation of curriculum is a parody; it cannot be achieved. If you wish to tell teachers what to do, you have no sanctions, you have no power ultimately to affect what happens in this classroom on this day. Even if you disapprove of what happens (and even if you can find what to disapprove of), you have no power of recrimination.

As soon as one recognises the realities of centralised reform one has to ask rather harder questions: is any reform to be, despite one's strongest wishes, merely on offer? If a reform is merely offered to the teaching profession, is this likely to produce change at the speed which society seems to demand? If one places new ideas in what is sometimes called the public domain, does this mean that we risk the misuse of ideas which have been carefully, rigorously and even faultlessly worked out? Are we bound, once a new educational idea stands within the public domain, to risk abuse?

If we are to deny the possibility of distortion and misuse, then we are almost bound to accept that local development work has greater significance. If this is so, then local work must be looked at in one of many ways. Is the management of curriculum change to be regarded as something which appeals to the teacher as a hobby? Is curriculum renewal to be regarded as something about which consciences must be searched – do teachers *always* have to decide on what is good and what is bad? Secondly, can reform be based on conceptions such as that some ideas are attractive and that others are repulsive? Should we accept, in the way that those who manage large corporations accept, that change, reform, progress and development are likely to be irrational? And if we enter into the realm of what is irrational, does this mean that we have to deny the professionalism of the teacher?

Local diffusion and reform

Since the impact of national policies has not yet been fully felt by schools in Britain no one can say how successful will be the idea that teachers themselves should be able to take over where national work leaves off. Certainly the theoretically defined aims of teachers' centres include emphasis on local development once the lead has been given by any centrally mounted development project. But teachers' centres do not yet provide local teachers with direct experience in curriculum-building. Teachers do, of course, come together in order to study, to appraise and to make the first range of decisions about the possible acceptance or rejection of ideas which have a national origin. But the leaders of teachers' centres are not bound to have either an experience or a skill in curriculum affairs. And certainly there is not yet any training for them in helping teachers to build anew.

If teachers are asked to do something the success of which depends on the *luck* of finding personal skills, interest, ingenuity and influence in the right quantity, in the right combination and in the right place when a change of curriculum is being contemplated, this hardly seems enough on which to base anything that we might call a national policy. The managers of change have, therefore, to recognise that the expression of hope in the early days of the Schools Council has already led to some confusion about how change should be handled. It might also lead to the moment when it is recognised that the things which can be achieved in the name of teacher-autonomy in Britain do not match the things that are claimed.

Signs are visible that teachers in England and Wales are already uneasy about the ambiguity of this autonomy. For instance, the National Union of Teachers at its annual conference in 1971 asked that a study should be made of the potentialities which lay in the idea of schools having staff councils who would be responsible for curriculum, school organisation, internal school finance and parent–teacher relationships. In the same year the results of an NUT study of the implications of teachers' participation in a variety of school activities began to be debated.

It is significant that a teachers' association should have reached this point after always having assumed the independence of teachers from external pressures. But the explanation which the NUT offered for this new concern centred on clear issues. Despite the legal responsibility and traditionally all-powerful image of the Heads of schools, five pressures towards greater participation by assistant teachers in the running of their schools began to be felt in the late 1960s. Collective teaching methods had developed within secondary schools at a time when they had grown markedly in the size and complexity of their organisation. Again, the rate of change within education had intensified to the point that a demand was created for the individual teacher to have a say in the way things were moving before it was all too late.

There was the point, too, that the idea of 'participation' had in general grown. This referred especially to participation of employees in the making of decisions which had previously been made only by employers – or participation of subordinates in things which had previously been determined by superiors. Insufficient recognition, the NUT felt, had been given to the assistant teacher's rights. The fifth point was that education should reflect movements in society at large. The pressure for a more active democracy could already be felt; it should be felt, too, within the schools.

Who has any power of management?

Any attempt to distinguish the strategies of development which are being devised by English-speaking countries leads to attention being drawn to the directions from which change is controlled. In Britain the claim is strongly made that responsibility lies primarily and constantly in the hands of teachers. In the United States and Canada it is assumed that change is effectively directed mainly in a downward direction, through the hierarchy of statuses. Central administration, at the American level of a state and at the Canadian level of a province, has to be the first to make any move in changing the face of teaching. In Britain, in contrast, no one would openly admit that *any* change could start elsewhere than in the classroom – in one classroom, from which the influences are felt, ripple-like, in a larger and larger number of schools.

The differences are, of course, responsible for the varying degrees of emphasis which countries put on theory and practice, on policies and on people. But between schools themselves in England and Wales there are different stresses, too. What starts in one classroom may get no further if it is stifled by the influence of the Head or of senior staff. If, however, these positively promote the initiative of ideas, the news of change travels faster.

Against this background, the fact that a major teachers' union has started to examine the participation by assistant teachers in the organisation of schools will be particularly significant if it leads us to re-examine some of our over-simple definitions of power within a school. As one Head says when he speaks of his relationship to the staff, his position is too easily described as that of the simple autocrat; it is quickly forgotten how far he can be affected by the influences of deputies, heads of department, long-experienced teachers, school secretaries, parents, caretakers and others.

One Head (Edward Blacksell in *The Head in the secondary school*, 1969) said that in the matter of communications he had over a period of ten years attempted to communicate with staff by means of staff meetings, conducted in the manner of the 'received law', in the manner of committee procedure, in the manner of small sectional discussions with group leaders. 'On all occasions the meetings have resulted in gleaming pearls of wisdom which dissolve in the school yard on a wet Friday afternoon. Those who hardly need a staff discussion are there to carry out, and they do carry out, the ideals of their chosen profession with a devotion which amazes me. But there are some who are merely time-servers; very often they do not know they are time-servers but their standards have never been tried and tested in any critical situation. They realise that they have security of tenure and are just not there to take their share of the burden.'

The same Head has also tried to communicate (by means of papers circulated to the staff) the purpose of encouraging them to think more deeply about what they were doing in school and to contribute more purposefully to the education of the children in their care. 'Over the years I have evolved a system of suggestions for form periods on topics such as hygiene, safety, uniform, vandalism, school routine, manners, absences, money, and medical matters. The items for consideration in form periods are to do with the day-to-day administration; it is worthy of note that the curriculum seems not to play any part in these communications.'

On curriculum, a not unexpected note of despair creeps in: 'The syllabuses of work rest in the drawer of the Headmaster's desk as an allegedly overall curriculum philosophy; they remain as a revelation of the divine, rather than as working documents – despite the fact that attempts have been made to break down each syllabus into terminal sections and even into weekly stints. But the nature of the teaching pattern and of the day just does not allow for this amount of systemization.'

Since he wrote those words this particular Head has experienced something which is relatively new in the organisation and curriculum in England and Wales. His school, together with three others and a College of Further Education, have prepared for a style of secondary school organisation which is novel. Its novelty lies in the fact that four schools have agreed to have, as far as is possible, a common curriculum and a common examinations policy up to the age of sixteen. All the children in this area of one local education authority will be educated once they reach the age of sixteen in an institution which combines the options of further education with the traditional options of sixth form work.

When schools are organised on radically new lines, the need to reorganise curriculum is obvious. The attempt to combine what the jargon a decade or more ago described as a curriculum which would meet the needs of new sixth formers with a curriculum which meets traditional needs in terms both of schooling and of further education, faces very obvious problems. The originator of curriculum change finds himself forced into a position in which he has to do *something*. As a manager of change he has to be aware of how much power he has, how well he is going to be backed, how persuasive his arguments will be and – finally – he has to have some degree of confidence in the validity and quality of the changes for which he is responsible.

Responsibility in teachers' centres

Who is it who is responsible for quality? The natural answer, in England and Wales, is the Head of the school. Nevertheless, there was some acceptance of – or search for – responsibility in the late 1960s and early 1970s by those who lead curriculum development from within teachers' centres.

The fact that teachers' centres have an uncertain influence on curriculum is explained perhaps by the comment of one typical full-time Warden of a teachers' centre. When he traced the growth of teacher attendances and the growth of the number of meetings which were organised at his centre over a period of eighteen months, he noticed that while the number of teacher attendances had more than doubled and that the number of separate meetings had *almost* doubled, the involvement of those teachers in the area who came from *secondary* schools was more or less negligible. He accounted for this by pointing out that their involvement in the work of a teachers' centre was slight because of the pressures which had been placed upon them by the organisation of their own schools. (It is to this reorganisation and to these pressures that the same Head who had, earlier, been quoted as being somewhat despairing about curriculum development, had referred. Thus, in a fairly typical area of one county where many things happen at the same time, it seems natural that teachers should first pay attention to their own institutions and only secondly to the broader demands of educational improvement at large.)

Contrast, then, the school and the teachers' centre: teachers' centres are claimed to be the main agencies of development. It is within these centres that the main impetus of management is expected nowadays to reside. Those who are Wardens of these centres, on either a full-time or a part-time basis, are the managers. Do they have a proper job to do? Do they know how to manage change?

The Wardens of teachers' centres are not trained to cope with development or the management of change. Nevertheless, if one takes a more or less reasonable sample of the kind of centre which now exists in England and Wales for curriculum development, a picture emerges which shows the differing kinds of pressure, disappointment, optimism and constructiveness which can lay a basis for the future.

Take, for instance, a long-established centre which not only provides attractive residential facilities but which also forms an enclave in one of the country's few colleges which specialises in a particular range of subject specialisms. At this centre the number of in-service training courses, conferences, seminars and workshops has doubled in five years.

What is particularly significant is that while work which is a separate concern of teachers in primary and secondary schools has increased gradually and steadily, the combination of primary and secondary work has increased very dramatically. This does not reflect any significant local movement in the organisation of middle schools but it does reflect a growing (and presumably national) preoccupation with the period which is now commonly described as the middle years of schooling. The establishment of comprehensive schools in greater numbers, the abolition of selection tests and of other procedures for separating children according to their abilities at the age of eleven – these movements have led to a clearer realisation of the continuous nature of education. One of the strongest forces for continuity is interconnection within the curriculum. The development of stronger lines of continuity is arduous but interesting for teachers who come new to the idea of their dependence upon each other. It is, however, helpful that many national development projects still offer a model of work which, in common with the earliest work which was launched by the Nuffield Foundation, covers the needs of pupils in the age-range of eight to thirteen years.

Another noticeable aspect of growth has, too, been the increase in the *type* of course and conference which teachers have attended. In five years, there are twice as many topics covered in the field of primary education; twice as many, too, in secondary education. The increase in the number of topics covered by both primary and secondary teachers together, however, shows a sixfold increase. The growth has, in each case, stemmed from the addition of courses which cover broad topics as well as single subjects. This again illustrates the gradual breakdown of separatism in British education. Not only are the stages of education coming to be more clearly seen to be linked but so also are the subject matters and disciplines of education.

In contrast, in one part of an education authority where (because of topography and tradition) teachers have been accustomed to isolation, another teachers' centre shows a comparable increase in the generalised type of course. This centre, although it has had the longest-serving full-time Warden, is still less than ten years old. In that time, however, it has passed through three phases: first, what was provided was the instructional type of course which teachers asked for simply to reduce their ignorance. The effects of metrication in British life and the changeover to metric measures at school was a clear example of this kind. New developments in the teaching of reading, new approaches to the humanities, the improvement of careers and counselling services, how best to use various new types of audio-visual aid – each of these found, in the early days, a strong following. Gradually, however, teachers came to feel that there were too many instructional courses. Two strains became apparent: first, an adult has only a limited capacity (or patience) for being taught rather than for devising something for himself. Secondly, the repetitious demand for attendance at courses week by week created an increasing lethargy.

At this point the description was invented of teachers being 'over-coursed'. A demand developed for more semi-autonomous study groups. The focus of effort moved from the extrinsic to the intrinsic domain. Teachers still asked for information and for (some) instruction; for the rest, however, they preferred to learn for themselves, under good guidance and with good support.

But what did guidance or support amount to? Successful groups (to quote the Warden of this centre) were characterised by having, first, a clear purpose or common interest (e.g. to identify the functions of the careers teachers or the characteristics of various reading schemes), secondly, an energetic and knowledgeable leader/secretary, and – third – administrative support where needed. This was the order of importance.

The same Warden went on to describe how these factors differently affected primary and secondary school teachers, how they differed in their intensity in work which had a continuous thread (for example, the development of methods of team teaching) as against efforts which were short-lived or had one straightforward purpose. The first two characteristics (a clear sense of purpose and energetic leadership) were seldom found in *ad hoc* groups of primary teachers. The success of, for instance, team-teaching seminars seemed attributable to the fact that Heads were concerned about how to make effective use of staff when limitations of space had prevented their using the traditional class-teacher type of organisation; secondly, one very able Head seemed to the group to have workable solutions for a wide range of detailed problems – and this mattered a great deal. Thirdly, the Warden was himself able to attend all meetings and to work with the Heads who were involved. It was possible to produce detailed minutes of meetings for subsequent study.

The so-called practicality of this kind of comment shows what the local success of curriculum development may depend upon. If you can bring people together, if you can persuade them to take some of the abstractions of education seriously, if you can recall what it is that they choose to express about these abstractions, then there is a chance that you will have something upon which to build.

It was not surprising that the Warden of this same teachers' centre reported that over eighteen months he had had to organise a substantial number of single meetings – that is, meetings which were not part of a continuous course. Most such meetings had no obvious follow-up in terms of subsequent work but were intended to enable ideas, information and examples of work to be given in a 'presentation'. Subsequently it was hoped that these might be taken up by a small group or in individual schools or classrooms. This did in fact happen. Such meetings became the staple of truly local centre-work where the limited number of teachers who were interested made it impossible to think in terms of broader courses or of specialised group work for which teachers came to a larger regional centre.

The effect of single meetings which lead to a proliferation of smaller scale and more localised efforts of teacher-initiated work is in itself interesting. The particular Warden who made these comments covers a broad geographical region of one LEA. But within that region there were in addition to the centre from which the Warden principally worked, smaller country towns with their own population of teachers who found it easier and possibly more congenial to work together on the basis of a small cell (or family) of professionals.

In commenting on the changes in attitude towards (and acceptance of) curriculum change which he noticed at this one teachers' centre, the same Warden pointed out that the relative success of different organisational approaches was only quantifiable in terms of teacher attendances. This brings us back to the difference in impact which can be made on local development work by official changes in the organisation of schools – in contrast with voluntary and less highly organised work which is taken on by certain teachers simply in pursuit of their own interests and professionalism.

The reorganisation of schools takes up the time and energy of teachers; this in itself is a useful sign of the benefit which the admittedly brief tradition of teachers' centres has brought to the profession. The teacher who has to face the reorganisation of his own school – and who has no choice about it – is more ready than he would have been a decade ago to assume that change in the shape of schooling requires also a change in the shape of education. It is this value principally which local development work has brought to the renewal of education in England and in Wales.

Thus reorganisation in itself calls for a considerable degree of curriculum replanning. But if teachers had not been used to the *idea* – even if they had previously done nothing about it – of being responsible for their own development work, for their own schools' curricula and for their own subjects' syllabuses, the formal reorganisation of schooling would be unlikely to be accompanied by the same degree of professional self-awareness as we nowadays see.

In contrast, another teachers' centre which is near to the headquarters of its own local education authority and which is also fairly near to a university, to an Institute of Education and to professional libraries, reflects the same pattern of movement away from specific and instructional courses for teachers to rather more generalised activities on the part of teacher groups.

In the context of curriculum improvement, it is worth paying attention to enquiries, researches, questions and uncertainties which are expressed by a number of teachers. In the centre which is described here, for instance, the Warden suggests that if there are improvements in the confidence which is now felt in the process of curriculum development then it is because of his own increasing awareness of what his job is, because of growth of experience on the part of the local executive committee, of teachers with and through whom he works, because of a growing and general awareness that what teachers themselves want is important (rather, perhaps, than what others think they need) and because of the growing acceptance of what teachers' centres can achieve – which amounts, mainly, to an awareness on the part of teachers and their employers (and of other agents) of the potentials of professional retraining.

This particular Warden suggested, for instance, that teachers' centres had to pass through a process of development which could not be artificially shortened. The first stage was that of catering for rudimentary needs ('tips for teachers') and of attempting inappropriate in-service techniques (which amounted to copying existing provision). Then a centre began to develop an identity of its own – and its role became clearer. Teachers became more actively involved as they learned to dispense with authoritarian leadership. As the surface needs of teachers became gratified, they became more aware of deeper needs – the need to examine critically what and why they were teaching. From this stage, the Warden prophesied that teachers would go on to want to examine critically the curriculum as a whole, and from that point to take a critical look at the system of education, as far as possible, in its entirety.

This kind of comment is optimistic: it reveals that teachers see that the process of curriculum change has implications for the totality of education and not simply for their own subject teaching, or for their own age-range or for their own specialism.

It can easily be said that education in England and Wales suffers because the teacher in the classroom sees his pupils day by day but sees the whole panorama of education very seldom. The possibilities which are offered by well-managed systems of curriculum development include the chance that the teacher who is preoccupied with particularities may see the wood rather than the trees, he may see a panorama rather than the microcosm which is his own professional world. It would not be too extravagant to claim that the success of local development of curriculum depends very much upon the confidence and optimism which teachers engender within themselves because they know what education, as a whole, is about rather than because they are satisfied with their daily work with small groups of children in separated and isolated schools.

The educative society of the professional teacher was an ideal which lay behind the report of the McNair Committee when Area Training Organisations were established. All the educational needs of an area were, if possible, to be met. All the education which was to be provided in one region was to have professional interest paid to it in terms of training, support, guidance and inspiration.

How far the ideals of the McNair Report in 1947 have found their reflection in the development of teachers' centres is something which we can still only guess at. When teachers' centres operate at their best, we can be fairly certain that the ideal of professional self-renewal is working. When teachers' centres, however, concern themselves with trivialities, with the outward forms of reorganisation and with those parts of curriculum development which are merely technical, merely instrumental, or merely concerned with the procedure of teaching, then we can be fairly certain that the local pattern of curriculum development is not succeeding.

Summary

The connection between national strategies of curriculum development and local effort reveals the distance, to some degree, between the abstract thinker and the daily practitioner. Because of the tradition of utilitarianism, as well as of pragmatic public activity deeply rooted in the English way of doing things, no one need be particularly surprised at the separation between theory and practice. The gap in fact is far shorter in England and Wales than it might be in some other countries. The planner, the abstract thinker, the researcher, each of these pays far greater respect, one feels, to the practising teacher within the British system than has been, by tradition, paid in other educational systems.

It may be that respect for practice and for the dailiness of the teacher's activity has been overemphasised. It may be that the English, as in other parts of Western Europe or across the Atlantic, should be more concerned with the purity of their plans and of their theories than with the way in which things can actually happen.

Whatever may be the philosophic rights or wrongs of the English way of doing things, however exasperating it may seem to the outsider that they should pay so much attention to practice and so much less respect to theory, nevertheless the problem of curriculum development and the problem of its management centres mainly on the polarity of ideas about practice and about centralisation, or about local activity, daily teaching and abstract philosophy. The next chapter will examine the degree to which the British system has within it some intrinsic weaknesses which may well prevent systematic curriculum development from ever reaching its proper fulfilment.

6 The obstruction of development

To manage curriculum development needs, first, an awareness of what has gone before: a sense of history encourages humility and may help the reformer to avoid brashness. Then, the manager has to know who nowadays has the strongest influence in shaping curriculum. He has to know, too, who those are who can most actively and purposefully involve themselves in the process of improvement. But he has also to be clear about the motives of those who desire change and about the limitations within which they work. Not least he has to have skill in recognising what he himself is handling, in recognising his own deficiencies and in discerning the points at which national, local, and school based initiatives for improvement can be best used.

Justifying improvement

Behind the outward pattern of good management lies the need to have good reasons for aiming at improvement at all. In one sense the Head of a school himself does not necessarily have to have very clear personal reasons for desiring improvement. For instance, in the secondary school he can leave both the organisation and the justification of change to his senior colleagues and to his heads of department: he himself need perhaps only touch the reins lightly and infrequently. In the primary school, admittedly, he has to show his hand more obviously; the smaller the school the greater his part will be. But whether the school is large or small, whether it is a primary school or a secondary school (or a middle school) it will not be long before the quality of the Head's concern for curriculum improvement becomes obvious.

The meaning of curriculum has to be clear to the Head: we have already seen how this clarity can be obscured in the secondary school by the need to organise things around a number of separate subjects. In the primary school, curriculum can be more readily defined without these obscurities. The curriculum is made up of those things which it is intended that the child shall learn. We leave the larger abstractions; once we reach the school's level of daily concern with curriculum, it is the teacher whose intention must lie behind its shape. Because there has to be intention, there then has to be a plan which marks out what should be learned and which gives reasons to justify what it is hoped that the children *will* learn. This justification requires that someone should define what the aims are of learning this in preference to that and that someone should, too, define the best ways of reaching those aims.

There will be few Heads who are so confident with the language of educational objectives that they will be able very readily to lay out the plans and the justifications which underpin their schools' curriculum. Some will argue that the language of educational objectives is, in any case, the wrong language because it compels us to talk as though education had separable ends and as though curriculum was, again, a separated set of means to those ends. It may be preferable for these people to say that the curriculum of a school is itself the expression of that school's purposes: the means and the end are one and the same thing.

To the question of justifying any particular policy of curriculum, however, the more common reaction will be *some* kind of reference to a set of objectives. Unfortunately, the ways in which Heads are prone to describe such objectives are likely to be familiar: most frequently schools will have only a rather vague statement of philosophy and of goals for everything that is taught. The so-called philosophy is rarely rigorous enough to serve as a criterion in deciding what should or should not happen in the school. The more vague the ideas, the easier it is to substitute one justification for another.

The uncertainty of a head teacher

In his own defence the Head, when he is questioned, is likely to refer to the absence of agreement about the purposes of education. He can see this as something which is logically connected with his own exercise of professional freedom, claiming that schools have the right to have differing objectives which they need justify only to themselves. Alternatively, the Head can argue that in a society where there is no explicit agreement about the purposes of education, questions about the objectives of individual schools should not be asked. He may say that interest in the purposes of schooling is, in any case, fairly new and that it should basically relate to those human values which society seeks to encourage. He may indeed go further and point out the obvious truth that ideas about the good life or about the quality of society are, at the least, elusive and difficult to agree about. In the context of general uncertainty why should schools be singled out for this questioning?

The Head who takes the argument to this level of generalisation is on fairly safe ground: we must all agree with his thesis about uncertainty and about the lack of social consensus about the purposes of education. Nevertheless, values are something with which we have day-to-day contact and about which education is bound to be (continually and in a practical way) concerned. Even if we cannot get rid of the impurities of uncertainty, we still have to make a stab at answering specific questions: why do the children of this school follow this curriculum? What are the intentions which lie behind it?

Common and frank answers – if the children were themselves asked – would be that they were learning this or that because they had to, or because they wanted to please their teacher, or because they felt they needed it in order to get on well with the next stage of their education or because their parents expected them to. For the teacher who felt that curriculum should be thoroughly child-centred these responses would not be good enough. He might suggest, indeed, that a certain curriculum should not be followed at all.

Anyone who took this view would prefer answers which justified a curriculum by reference to its interest or its capacity to enhance the learner's life. The teacher who would support this would, for instance, expect children to want to learn things in order to be able to understand themselves, and the world, better.

The ease with which it is possible to justify a child-centred curriculum needs no detailed comment here. It is enough to say that it is well-known how liberal, progressive and professionally good-hearted it is to place the learner at the centre of the educational universe. But because it is so acceptable, it carries also the risk of plans which are not thorough, of methods which may serve aims which have too short a view. And it can belie the idea that curriculum is indeed made up of 'intended learnings' – for it can be questioned what part the teacher has to play in a scheme of learning where the justification rests in the interest of the child rather than in fulfilling the aims and intentions of any adult.

Frameworks for improvement: the school

It is, then, fairly complicated for the Head either to justify his wish to improve curriculum or in this way to lay the basis of good management. Two of his particular difficulties will be personal ones: the Head is known to his staff, he is known as a certain kind of person, as a thinker or as a guesser, as one who imposes a plan or who seeks agreements. If he tries to use justifications which are unusual, those who are familiar with him will assume that he has borrowed an unknown language in order to clothe or even to conceal something new. He is unlikely to be thought of as having taken up a new way of thinking in any thoroughgoing sense. In fact, unless his staff have seen a Head going through the process of being converted to a new view they will not believe that any conversion has taken place. The words are new but the man is the same.

The second difficulty has to do with the kind of people assistant teachers are: if they are energetic in their thinking, if they read, reflect, watch their own teaching and can analyse its strengths and weaknesses, then they will have some of the right equipment with which to help in the management of an improvement. If they are good teachers, too, and have the interest and sympathy of their pupils, their equipment should be complete. But the training of teachers and their selection and appointment for particular schools need not be connected either with their personal style nor, altogether, with their professional competence. Hence the assistant teacher's view about the purposes of curriculum and about the choice of methods to achieve those purposes will be something which will be highly personal unless it is possible to create some unity of ideas with other people.

There are two extremes: at one end curriculum is the product of a number of different and highly personal views. At the other extreme it is an imposed idea, coming from one source. The problem is that of avoiding the extremes. One solution is to depersonalise the giving of orders and to unite everyone in studying the problem, in discovering 'the law of the situation' and in obeying that law.

Another approach is that of creating a scheme of organisation and a structure which is based on principles – principles which take priority over personalities. This, to some minds, is in the long run better for morale and indeed for the happiness of individuals. If things go wrong those who are affected can preserve their anonymity and can blame the system rather then themselves – and they therefore prefer impersonality to an organisation which is built around persons.

Another view of management is the acceptance that organisations do *not* make decisions. The purpose of an organisation is to provide a framework in which decisions can be made in an orderly manner. A school is not, of course, simply a machine for making policy but it does itself have an organisation which is concerned with the planning of curriculum and with providing a framework in which decisions can be made logically, coolly and in accordance with principles which are shared.

By this interpretation the Head is not someone who simply touts ideas in the effort to discover how much agreement he can win for them. He is the one who sees to the setting-up of a structure of consultation and discussion: the structure has to be handled by everyone in a certain way lest it be pulled apart and fail to do its job. There have to be rules for handling the structure. Assistant teachers must know how much time they have when they are asked to formulate an opinion, they must know how thoroughly they need to be able to defend their opinions, they must know whether they can expect a decision to emerge from a conflict of opinions, whose job it is to resolve conflict and how firmly a decision must be maintained once one is made.

Within a framework which both assistant teachers and the Head can see and understand, decisions about curriculum become intelligible and defensible. The origin becomes visible of those ideas which have to be managed to the point of action.

If the curriculum is to be pupil-centred or adult-directed, if it is to be based on techniques, for instance, which are connected with individualised learning or to be based on instruction, all those in the school will know at least where it began. Everyone will know when it was that he had an opportunity to take an initiative or to make some formative contribution. He will know, too, when the chance will come again, how the progress of an idea will be assessed, who is to assess it and when. In this way, even if personal interest or the commitment to improve things or energy for reading, for reflection and for self-analysis – even if these are felt only at a fairly low level by the Head and by his assistants, nevertheless much can be achieved simply through the existence of a *framework* which tells people the rules of when to act, what the limits of their activity should be and what outcome can be expected.

Out-of-school

The largest framework for curriculum development outside schools in England and Wales is provided by the Schools Council: it, too, has created its rules. People are gradually getting to know what to expect and what to do.

Some of the origins of the Council have been described; its current work is well-chronicled (in, for instance, annual reports). Less well-known are the ways in which the trial stages of major projects in curriculum development expand into stages of dissemination and then, after final modification and publication, into the stage of diffusion. Most has so far been written about the Humanities Curriculum Project: this started as a materials-producing project which rapidly discovered the need to become a project which was also concerned with changing the methods and organisation of teaching. Projects which changed rather less in the process of evolution were those which were concerned with modern languages, sciences (at various levels of sophistication), mathematics and school technology. The first three of these subject areas have not yet had chroniclers to record their processes of change. However the last of them, in technological studies, has been a project mainly concerned with describing and widely publicising new work which would otherwise have had an impact on only a limited number of pupils.

That a development project can be considered by many to be most successful when it simply concerns itself with the better *communication* of ideas to local teachers rather than with invention and the development of teaching materials, is itself interesting enough to raise the question of whether the development of curriculum needs predominantly to be a matter of creating new content or of devising new methods. Development could, quite respectably, be defined as the development of *awareness* or of *interest* in new ways of teaching amongst a steadily increasing number of teachers. Good communication could, in fact, be enough.

An emphasis on good communication is not shared by all the national projects of the Schools Council. Indeed anyone who looks in detail at the Council's index of project profiles must be surprised by the large number of obscure projects which even at a date which was later than their official ending had still published no report, conclusions or even interim findings.

To some extent, the obscurity of some national projects is strange and disappointing. It contradicts the spirit of those early working papers of the Council which have already been referred to; there, the hoped-for role of teachers' centres had been described. Good communication was, in the early days, given high importance. The Council was said to exist to promote a process of which the essential element was the offer of help to teachers to examine the objectives of curriculum as a whole and of subjects in particular. Help was also to be offered to schools in the development and trial use of methods and materials which were judged most likely to achieve the objectives which teachers agreed upon. Assessment of success and the feedback of findings were also to be supported.

Each of these tasks needed a clear and confident relationship between project development teams, trial school areas, and teachers' centres at large. Teachers' centres in particular had to form part of a carefully meshed network of communication; they were – in theory – set up to focus local interest, to provide places where teachers could share criticisms and questions about curriculum and where they could be given help by their local education authorities or by their nearest University Institute of Education. Communication on its own could provide, in these terms, almost an entire framework for the development of curriculum.

However, it is not usually accepted as a sufficient *strategy* for change simply that new ideas should have currency, that people should argue and disagree, or that information should pass freely from the shapers of central projects to teachers – or from school to school. Strategies have to be built around an effort to change attitudes. They have to be purposeful. Those who conceive strategies of change are unlikely to think that communication is, really, enough. Because of this, each major national project of curriculum *development* (as opposed to projects which are basically tasks of research and survey) has linked with it a scheme of in-service training. This will be examined in the next chapter. But in the meantime, are there any morals which we can draw from experience in England and Wales, within about a decade, about the relationship between centralised plan and local action?

Can we claim to know enough about the nature of resistance to change to be able to point to any practicable development of policy?

National ideals and local resistance

When, in the previous chapter, a picture was drawn of the national plan for curriculum development in England and Wales, a reference was made to differences of response.

In the attempt to draw some conclusions about the ways in which national change might produce different responses, six questions were asked, the first of which was 'How is a decision made about the subject areas which need reform?' Although the attempt to answer this question has already been made, it may now be more useful to ask a subsidiary question instead of concentrating attention simply on how or why a decision is made nationally and who makes it. It would, for instance, be worthwhile to find out whether anybody takes into account how attractive or how credible or how useful a nationally conceived idea might be in circumstances which were entirely local – in, that is, a particular school and in a particular classroom.

The literature of resistance to change is broad in its coverage and comparatively well-known in its relevance to innovation. The way in which administration of change in education is resisted has been chronicled largely in Canada and the United States but also now, through the work of the Centre for Educational Research and Innovation, in Western Europe as well. Basically, resistance is not something simple. It is a mixture quite often of ignorance and misunderstanding or of belief that things from an earlier time which were already outmoded can still survive. To accompany the difficulty and sense of frustration – all of which is part of the environment of resistance – there are inevitably references to the burdensome nature of organising so many of the things which have to precede change or resentment of the different conditions of work which accompany change. Development, novelty, change and innovation, all these things bring also some challenge to the boundaries of authority. People have to work out whether the old way of doing things had any particular sanction attached to it. If new boundaries are to be defined, then those who wish to manage the development of curriculum or indeed of anything else that is new within education have to take account of the considerable resistance which many teachers will put up to the abandoning of traditional boundaries. People know their place within the system of education. To alter that position is irksome and also can give rise to fear.

None of this is particularly new; the reminiscences of Her Majesty's Inspectors of schools and of those who have been involved locally either as members of the clergy or as inspectors with local authorities or, more rarely, as administrators with the same type of local authority, have put on record the degree of misunderstanding which can arise quite simply between those who are more sophisticated in education and those who concentrate their efforts on the local benefit of particular communities.

There are stories in plenty about the ways in which Her Majesty's Inspector visiting a village school on summer's day used to question children about the insects, blossoms, fruits, or other signs of natural life which surrounded the rural school. Children in remote south-western villages would use traditional names for animals or birds. HMI would find this unattractive or amusing. Occasionally Inspectors of Schools would take it upon themselves to condemn what they felt to be the misuse of words. They would assess local usages as quite simply 'wrong'. There were differences, therefore, quite simply between the language which people spoke according to some national norm (that which was recognised, perhaps, by the Board of Education or even by those who preceded the Board) and the language which was spoken as a living thing day by day in our schools at the turn of the century and even later.

In reverse, Inspectors could ask children to define dodecahedra and isosceles triangles; they could ask children to name the highest peak in Africa; they could ask how high it was; they could ask which rivers drained Siberia. According to particular styles of centralised curriculum, children could give answers to these quite sophisticated questions. On the other hand they were unable to name flowers, trees, birds and insects which were found in the school playground and in the surrounding fields. The idiocy of this type of misunderstanding between those in positions of central authority in education and those who were the practitioners in particular villages and small communities far away from London was and always has been obvious. Just as it is presumptuous for anyone to assume that a common language is shared between towns and villages, between highly educated and comparatively uneducated people, so also it is presumptuous – and always has been – to assume that the things that are required by society to be taught to children are over-closely connected with their daily life. The question is whether it is more shameful for a child not to know the name of a particular tree or whether he only gives it the name which those in his particular locality would give it.

Admittedly parochial examples of misunderstandings such as these are nowadays more rare than they would have been thirty, forty or fifty years ago. Nevertheless they still represent the kind of gross misunderstanding which can exist between those who stand at the centre of things and those who work at the periphery.

There is no need to bring into play at this point complicated references to models of change. We are not talking about over-sophisticated social and organisational patterns of development; far more simply one has to acknowledge that the development of anything that is new in education has to depend very largely on the degree to which the teacher can actually understand what is being said by those who wish to create novelty. If the teacher does understand and understands without fear or without sensing that the thing is really too complicated to be grappled with, then, there is some chance that innovation and development can go ahead with comparatively little resistance. On the other hand, if the teacher feels that the thing is too complicated, too new or too revolutionary, then resistance is bound to be higher.

This statement of the obvious does not, of course, take into account the degree to which teachers prefer, from time to time, to take the easy way out. What is more comforting than to suggest that not only is the newly developed idea difficult to understand but also that it is inappropriate, over-complicated and too sophisticated to be relevant to the needs of particular pupils in a particular area? This latter position does after all represent something like the view of those who wish to protect children from change which is engendered by people who are described as mere theoreticians. The education of children is related, in these terms, to their own highly localised environment. What the outside world or the larger world might propose as a better or more up to date basis of education is rejected because it does not apply here and now to these children, to this class and to these homes.

Beyond this over-simple description of one type of resistance to change there are others which will be described in later chapters. It is enough here to notice that the degree of misunderstanding which can exist between those who work centrally and those who work locally has been chronicled not only in reminiscences of inspectors and others but also in official reports. In, for instance, the Plowden Report (1967) there was a very clear statement about the way in which the activities of nursery schools and many infants schools were misunderstood. Accusations that children were wasting their time in school, that they were playing instead of working were noted by the Plowden Committee. It had to be pointed out, even in 1967, that the distinction between work and play for younger children and possibly for older children and adults too was artificial. The Committee noticed that in essence people's understanding of what play and work were actually made up of took its origin from old ideas. School hours were equated with work, that which was done out of school was equated with play. But, said Plowden, it is well-known how play – in the sense of 'messing about' either with material objects or with other children or of creating fantasies – was vital to children's learning. It was therefore vital in school. The Report went to the point of saying that adults who criticised teachers for allowing children to play were unaware that play is the principal means of learning in early childhood.

This kind of certainty of statement represents the type of message which can be passed to one professional by another. The Plowden Report was speaking to teachers; but it was also speaking to those who lay on the edge of, or even completely outside, education. It acknowledged the continuing resistance which would be experienced by teachers even to ideas and methods which are very well established. But simply by restating revered principles of learning the Plowden Report did nothing to help teachers and others who are responsible for the education of young children to help *outsiders* to understand why their mistrusts were unfounded.

Even earlier, in 1931, the Hadow Report on the primary school had stressed how curriculum was to be thought of in terms of activity and experience rather than of knowledge to be acquired and facts to be stored. Although this was said again in 1967, the Plowden Report must have the same effects as Hadow; it assumes that official reports and commentaries are preaching to those who can be converted.

This in itself is not very useful to the job of managing innovation. It does not take into account the views of those who press, each day, more closely upon the teacher; it does not take into account the fact that teachers have to do things which are intelligible not only to the children whom they teach but also to the parents of those children. Therefore if play and messing about are difficult to disentangle, then it is the job of those who advocate more play, or more learning through play, to ensure that the outside world knows what is being done.

The Plowden Report admittedly recognised this when, rather briefly, it pointed out that the interest in learning which children show (as well as an *urge* to learn) is affected by the attitude of parents as well as by teachers. Plowden pointed out with no great originality that apathy would result when children's parents showed little interest or clamped down on children's curiosity and enterprise – or told them constantly not to touch things. It was equally bad if parents didn't answer children's questions. Children easily learned how to be passive from a teacher who allowed them little scope in managing their own affairs. Teachers who relied, too, only on instruction or who forestalled children's questions or who answered them too quickly – instead of asking the further question which would set the children on the way to their own solution – were accepted as being likely to lead children to be disinclined to learn.

The wording of this kind of message in the Plowden Report is very reasonable. It relates resistance, misunderstanding and the difficulty which attends the acceptance of new ideas to human factors about motivation, inclination, intelligence, or the capacity to change one's ways. It is significant in that it gives a warning that the externals of innovation are important, certainly; but more important are those factors which are deeply embedded in the process of learning and which are directly relevant to the task of improving children's *chances* of learning. It is also a message which points out that the teacher alone is not the arbiter of the effectiveness of novelty; unless the purpose behind what is new is related to the expectations which a child's parents have of his schooling, then the introduction of change is almost bound to fail. The teacher cannot battle with the attempt to understand what is new at the same time as he is trying to explain the purposes of innovation to those who have a more direct and constant contact with his pupil.

Another kind of difficulty which was noticed in the Plowden Report also throws light on the division which exists between local practice and national plans. In its comments on present-day conceptions of timetabling in primary schools, the Report pointed out that ideas about the so-called free day, the integrated day and the integrated curriculum were comparatively recent. The changes implied in any view of a flexible curricular pattern represented a revolution from the type of timetable which local education authorities had, until quite recently, expected schools to prepare. Heads were expected to show exactly what each class was doing during every minute of the week and to provide a summary showing the total number of minutes to be spent on each subject. In extreme cases, the curriculum was divided into spelling, dictation, grammar, exercises, composition, recitation, reading, handwriting, tables and mental arithmetic. It was obvious, the Report thought, that this arrangement was not suited to what was known about the nature of children, or about the classification of subject matter or about the art of teaching.

This in itself is enough to reveal how tardily local education authorities abandoned their loyalty to requirements which had their origin, as we have already seen, in the early years of this century. And it may be that bureaucratic attitudes are in any case more resistant to change than the professional attitudes of teachers, advisers and inspectors. But in time, resistances weaken. People are won over by argument, worn down by the effort of fighting or gently moved from a state of apathetic reluctance to one of grudging acquiescence in what is new.

Confusions and misuse

The management of change in curriculum seems inevitably to face one particular kind of unwilling resistance in the form of not understanding what the exercise of development is about. If there is confusion or misunderstanding, where does it spring from?

W. Kenneth Richmond (*The school curriculum*, 1971) culled from one journal four statements which defined curriculum. Each came from a British professor of education who had contributed a great deal to the work of clarifying ideas about curriculum. Their definitions of curriculum go like this:

> All the learning which is planned and guided by the school, whether it is carried on in groups or individually, inside or outside the school (John Kerr).

> That the curriculum consists of content, teaching methods and purpose may in its rough and ready way be a sufficient definition with which to start. These three dimensions interacting are the operational curriculum (Philip Taylor).

> A programme of activities designed so that pupils will attain, as far as possible, certain educational ends or objectives (Paul Hirst).

> The contrived activity and experience – organised, focused, systematic – that life, unaided, would not provide. It is properly artificial, selecting, organising, elaborating, and speeding up the processes of real life (Frank Musgrove).

These definitions differ in their degree of complication. The definitions quoted from Kerr and Hirst are perhaps misleadingly simple. Taylor's draws attention to the philosophical distinction between an *extensive* definition ('What is curriculum?': 'This thing that I can demonstrate here is what I call curriculum') and an *intensive* definition ('What is curriculum?': 'Curriculum is a set of ideas which can be adapted for differing pedagogic purposes: adaptations of the pattern of ideas need always to be controlled by a clarity about objectives, clarity about how to reach those objectives and a determination progressively to evaluate how successful the process of trying to reach each objective really is'). Musgrove, by connecting the idea of an unavoidable artificiality about curriculum to the real life of the learner takes the intensive definition further: he prescribes what curriculum should, in his view, do. He does not pretend to describe it as it is.

Each time a teacher attends any form of in-service training about curriculum – whether it has to do with separated subject-content, method or school organisation and management – he will be confronted at some point with a definition of curriculum. He will not always know whether it is a definition which he has to accept as a pre-condition of following the other arguments of, say, the lecture or seminar. He will not necessarily be clear whether he is being given a traditional definition which he should accept because the definition is already (but perhaps unknown to him) in common currency. But he may be equally unclear when someone produces a maverick definition which is personal and perhaps bizarre and which is intended to stimulate thought rather than, simply, to define.

Each time a teacher is uncertain about what faces him, he is properly cautious. Caution can either *look* like resistance or transform itself into purposeful resistance. The latter is most likely to happen when the teacher feels that he cannot accept or rationalise something which seems, in its presentation to him, to be an absurdity.

It is likely to be because he wants to avoid the risks and consequences of absurdity that the teacher will pay the greatest respect to demonstrations of successful practice by other teachers. Since the confidence engendered in avoiding absurdity is a major factor in thinning out resistances to new ideas, this reliance on the demonstration of other people's practical success has a considerable strategic value.

In addition to the variety of confusing definitions which he faces, the teacher also faces the sheer *size* of the thing called curriculum. For instance, in discussing the systems-analysis approach to curriculum, Richmond suggests that the larger is the system, the greater is the certainty that the sheer amount of information about it will be so overwhelming as to be unmanageable.

Those who are unlikely to be deterred by any problem of size or intelligibility will be the makers of conceptual models, the theorists, the cyberneticians. Such workers have little ambition to know the whole of any system – whether it is to do with education at large, with a limited sense of curriculum, with theory of learning, or, for instance, with developmental psychology. It is quite reputable to have the aim of achieving a knowledge of something which, although only part of the total picture, is nevertheless in itself complete for its own purposes. To the day-to-day practitioner the 'system' in systems-analysis then becomes not an atlas of the world but a route map. It makes direction-finding manageable and less confusing than it might otherwise be but the area which is covered can be too small and too specialised in its interest to be of broad value in making up any *strategic* understanding of curriculum development.

When, however, the management of curriculum makes things so simple that they appear to require no thought or to be capable of being accepted as truisms without further review, then other dangers arise; these are notably the dangers of misuse.

The Plowden Report described how there came to be a greater awareness of social problems in education during the 1939–45 war. One result was a plethora of books, descriptions and practical guides for teachers.

Most of these advocated one thing; for a brief time activity and child-centred education became dangerously fashionable. Misunderstandings jeopardised the progress which had been made by the so-called true pioneers.

Even so, misunderstandings were never as widespread in the schools themselves as might have been supposed by reading the press. They did not outweigh the gains which were notable in certain subject areas. Nevertheless, then as now, schools which continued on traditional lines to emphasise instruction exceeded the number of those which erred by excess of innovation. And in any case, as Plowden pointed out, correctives came in the shape of an emphasis on *quality* in the learning experiences provided for children – and on the positive function of the teacher.

The size of the problems which can occur in innovation may, then, cause sufficient dismay to trigger off resistance. To diminish this sense of dismay, the managers of innovation can attempt to simplify the problems and to provide intelligible route maps. But sometimes the search for intelligibility leads to oversimplification and to too ready and unexamined an acceptance of complex truths.

Sales resistance

If it seems unavoidable that models of the process of innovation tend to generalise and to oversimplify, this must be because of the inexhaustibly detailed picture which is produced when change is examined closely. The detail in each model has to be selected for its appropriateness to a particular purpose. In Britain innovators suffer from having to use other countries' models without a clear enough understanding of their original purpose.

Admittedly we may sometimes feel justified in asking whether the purpose of some models, even in their proper setting, was ever clear; but this is likely to be because they miss the flavour of the classroom. In aiming, too, at universality of application they often miss the nuances of negotiation which are needed with heads, with advisers, or with administrative officers who are willing but who have their hands full and who feel uncertain of their stance in unfamiliar fields of new curriculum or of organisational strategy. When they extend to analysing leadership and partnership many models appear to those in England and Wales – again perhaps because of their countries of origin – to describe situations in which the superordinate's *prescription* of curriculum is still a matter of the present or of the very recent past. And they miss something of the organic, self-modifying nature of the process of renewal.

But if models give us little help in the minutiae of the task of accelerating change and reappraisal in a particular school in a particular district, the familiar pictures of resistance tend, too, to be imprecise. The resistant figure is drawn as someone, generally, who conceives himself as being acted upon rather than as a participant in the process of change. He is no longer described as 'upward mobile', he separates himself in the cocoon of education from changes in the competitive outside world. He may go through the motions of change but he is unlikely to internalise any alteration in his manner of working. He is, if he is a teacher, accustomed to autonomy, to isolation in the classroom and to a more or less complete absence of pressures to undergo retraining. His response to the organisational environment of a school or college appears to lead to his conception of his role (the longer it is allowed to reinforce itself) as something which discourages him from taking risks. He will change his visible behaviour more readily than he will change his (less observable) attitudes. And those values which are centred on any gradually built-up system of professional belief will change even less readily.

In contrast to this grim catalogue, the person who handles innovation easily is the one who will fit well into a creative organisation. Any man is a paragon who can respond to the demands of an organisation which, in a composite definition, encourages men of ideas, has open channels of communication, encourages contact with outside sources, employs heterogeneous types of worker, assigns non-specialists as well as experts to problems, uses an objective, fact-founded approach, encourages evaluation of ideas on their merits rather than according to the status of the persons originating them, makes systematic efforts to select personnel and to reward them on the basis of merit, which experiments with new ideas instead of prejudging them, is decentralised and diversified in contrast to less innovative organisations, has an 'administrative slack' which permits time and resources to be used to absorb errors, has a risk-taking ethos, is not run as a 'tight ship' and is organisationally autonomous.

In a comprehensive inventory like this there are some elements which describe good schools – in any country. Most of those elements centre on ideas such as openness, risk-taking, freedom from outside pressures, and freedom, too, from hierarchical rigidities. Each of these elements represents a complex knot of attitudes and assumptions on the part of those who are involved in fostering change – but the sort of knot in which as you loosen some strands, others tighten.

Summary

The obstruction of development is something which will be felt more keenly at the level of a school's day-to-day operation than by those who are responsible for the dissemination of a nationally inspired reform.

It is the Head, the head of department and, in the end, the assistant teacher in a secondary school who will know how to create his own resistance to what is new or, conversely, how to circumvent resistance which is inspired by other people. The attempt has been made to show that both to create certain types of resistance and to overcome it is each, in its own way, a reputable form of activity.

There are few shared norms of professional behaviour to guide teachers who are faced with new developments. There is no tradition of highly organised resistance to change in England and Wales – but nor is there any historical picture of rapid and optimistic acceptance of change.

This chapter has touched on some of the difficulties which the manager of curriculum development will face both within school and in teachers' centres or other bases of new work which lie outside the walls of the school itself. Attention has been drawn to the variety of explanations and rationalisations which can be put forward in justification of resistance. Indeed, it can be shown that resistance is, often, too strong a word. Teachers, after all, do not like to look upon themselves as people who are out to defeat development or improvement or reform. They look upon themselves as guardians of what has been proved to be right, or good, or simply appropriate for pupils. To get behind the pretensions of this defence of standards and existing practice we have to look more closely at particular examples of school-based improvement. The following chapter will examine not only what can happen within a school but also the types of programme which teachers' centres can promote in order to avoid head-on resistance to novelty.

7 Local development: schools and teachers' centres

In thinking about hierarchy and freedom from pressure it is obvious that bureaucracy needs rules which are not simply those of control; procedural control and innovation appear incompatible. But the type of bureaucracy which *controls* activity will often be concerned, too, to give visibility to consequences of activity. While control in itself can stultify innovation, the necessity for visible results allows some evaluation to be attempted and allows those who make up each bureaucracy to encourage and to reward the successful innovator. By this argument, an orientation in a local authority, for instance, towards the simple control of activity, towards economic pay-off or towards formality in the relationships between administrators or inspectors and teachers in school is likely to have a negative effect on innovation. A positive effect is more likely to result from the light rein of liberalism.

At the risk of labouring the point, it is worth remembering that the kaleidoscope of authority patterns within the British school system can delude us at one moment into seeing it as the most liberal in the world, at others as a cynically erected structure of concealed prescription. The picture which one sees at any particular time markedly affects the view which is taken of the ease or difficulty of disseminating new thought.

If a wide variety of styles of authority and organisation defeats the purpose of models of change-management, it is equally true that the variety of modes and levels of resistance bedevils the attempt to draw pictures which are too simple. Confusing, too, are attempts to relate speed of dissemination to the characteristics of particular innovations. To some extent this confusion may be a result of the tendency of teachers not to be as concerned with specific results as with what has been called the professing of cultural patterns. This separation from specifics lies among the deeper reasons for difficulty about, and resistance to, improvement. Three other aspects of education – its vulnerability to the social environment, the professional self-image (with its associated values) of those within it and its diffuseness of goals – each of these mark it off as something so different from other types of profession that the language of management often has difficulty in finding the appropriate words.

The degree of resistance and facilitation which innovation will meet will differ according to what is being sold, who is selling it, his purpose in doing so, and the person to whom he is selling it. In English and Welsh primary schools new ideas in mathematics now seem to get over fairly quickly. Partly this results from a thirty year war of attrition by impenitent reformers, partly because new mathematics are, simply, a vogue, and partly because it is basically more interesting to teacher and child than the old stuff.

Language reform for the benefit of younger children seems more difficult: partly this must be because the current preoccupation has altogether more recent origins than the concern for new maths and partly because a close analysis of individual pupils' language development goes against the belief that free development is central to the education of infants. Partly, too, it may be more difficult because linguistics are themselves difficult to grasp. But also we cannot forget that language, reading, and English are easily confused. Old confidences, even if they are misplaced, are difficult to dislodge. The sociological justifications of an early concentration on language either point to all the battles having been lost before school age or challenge the teacher to deny that she has as nakedly a social role as this approach seems to require. To these two examples could be added a variety of guesses as to why the understanding of French in the junior school, of science for the eight year old, or of environmental studies for the older primary school age range each differ sharply from one another in the speed and effectiveness of their contribution to new curriculum.

In the secondary school a comparable tale is true: mathematics reform is comparatively straightforward within the limitations imposed by a shortage of specialist teachers, the humanities raise more difficult problems, religious education's reform meets with varying success, English seems unchangeable, sceince is renewing itself gradually – and so on. But despite the variety of responses certain factors seem repeatedly to apply to the fate of innovation in British schools. These relate to the role and work-style of the Head, of senior teachers, of inspectors and advisers, of official guidance given through in-service training or through publications.

The first focus of all influences is the Head. He is the leader of change or of resistance. Just as, perhaps, the most pitiful sight in the present-day secondary school is that of the authoritarian Head who has earlier reduced his staff to apathy and frustration, and who nevertheless wishes to catch up with modernity through this or that aspect of curriculum development, so the most testing task for the Head is the preservation of lively stability in his school. He has to avoid disruption but he has, too, to be prepared to live dangerously. How dangerously it is up to him to decide. Peter Snape has written (*The Head in the secondary school*, 1969) that the Head has to balance a number of functions, of organising the hunt for the school's objectives, of communicating his ideas not only to those within the school but also to the world outside, of evaluating the school's effectiveness, of developing his successors, of carrying out organisational repairs – and all the while acting as the prime 'innovation-and-ideas man'.

At root the most significant distinction in terms of managing what is new – as between Head, assistant teacher and adviser – appears to lie in the contrast between those who expect to be assessed by their success in keeping schools going smoothly and those whose best results lie in evidence of their vivacity, dynamism and open-mindedness. If this contrast is unavoidable it seems to mean that those who are directly involved in the applications of new work – that is directly with children – are only for part of the time talking the same language as those who form the school's next nearest contact with outside sources of innovation.

A primary school

How the school takes over an innovation has not yet, in Britain, been studied at any depth. But in one recorded example, Peter Evans (*Leadership in primary schools*, 1969) lays out the process in the fairly straightforward field of primary school mathematics. He describes his particular starting point as being, jointly, suggestions given by an adviser, the Head's forming of his own opinions from a period of observation, and the judgement, coldly made, that the subject area of maths needed a more systematic approach. Interestingly, however, a more diffuse judgement was reached by the Head at the same time, the judgement that his school with its predominantly working-class children needed a social as well as an instructional change. This was bound to be more diffuse because it in part depended upon temperament and in part upon an individual taste in professional reading. In this instance it was the reading of Josephine Klein which unlocked some thought as well as some practical planning about the connection between the significance of exploratory, participant and individualised learning and the effects of teaching method.

From then on the Head consulted and gained agreement from his staff that changes in the method of maths teaching were necessary. This was only a broad agreement – and having established the principle it was then up to the Head to establish the necessary facilities (for instance, a new maths workroom) and to carry out introductory sessions for his colleagues. The rather prescriptive position of the Head was expected by his colleagues, he alone had the appropriate experience for carrying out this type of innovation and, in his own view, it seemed more efficient to avoid the committee approach.

The next step was the reading of two basic papers by the staff, followed by attendance at a very short course of in-service training. An experiment of one new method was carried out and teachers from other schools witnessed it and commented upon it. These were useful as background but not for the detailed preparation which then had to be carried out by the Head – in terms of translating advice into action, of organising materials and spaces and of organising further in-school training sessions for the staff. New methods, when they were fully introduced, seemed to succeed not only with the children but also in eliciting spontaneous team-work from the teachers in another innovation which led to changing the social structure of the school and in giving the teachers the confidence and faith to interest and to instruct parents.

In the words of this Head:

> 'In a small way, this resembles the classic pattern of curriculum development. The researchers arrive at certain conclusions seen to be of educational significance. The educationist sieves these research findings (sometimes through further research) and presents ideas in a form which is, or should be, understandable and recognisably relevant to practitioners. The practical innovator translates the work of the educationist into techniques, methods and organisations capable of practical application in the school itself. The day-to-day practitioner modifies and adapts (or accepts) and uses the material with children.'

This example of a clearly directed innovation is still comparatively uncommon in British schools. The reason lies mainly in the wish to preserve those invisible boundaries which have already been described. Inertia helps the task of preservation (or the preservation of traditional boundaries produces inertia – it is not clear which); either way, too marked a concern for stability, for status quo and for dignities conferred by tradition sometimes hinders innovation.

The dissatisfaction of assistant teachers

The motives for being open-minded or the reverse have much to do with teachers' satisfactions in their jobs. Like most jobs the elements within them which are satisfying are connected with achievement, recognition, the attraction of the work itself, responsibility and advancement.

However, in contrast, anyone's dissatisfaction with his job does not stem from the absence of these things. People are dissatisfied with their jobs because of the policies (or non-policies) under which they have to work, because of the way in which they are supervised, because of how much they are paid, because of their personal relationships with those who work with them and because of their basic working conditions. Satisfaction and dissatisfaction are not, then, the opposites of each other but are concerned, rather, with two different ranges of any worker's needs. One range of needs is concerned with avoiding deprivations (physical and social); if these needs are not met, dissatisfaction follows. The other range of needs is concerned with achieving things and doing things well. If these *are* met, the job is a satisfying one.

Just as the idea has developed of what is called 'job hygiene' to describe the process of avoiding dissatisfactions, so the idea of what the jargon calls 'motivator factors' has been developed to describe the elements of any job which proves satisfying. The teacher who is faced with an offer of new materials or new methods will have that offer made within one or another of several definitions of curriculum. He will be exhorted to work out how the new idea will fit his purposes (after he has rethought those purposes). He will also be asked to be vigilant about the effects of the novelty if he decides to try it. Many of these demands will relate to some of the satisfying aspects of work – to achievement, to the attractiveness of the job, and to the question of professional responsibility. But when he is faced with the new demands which curriculum development can make, the teacher can also very naturally ask questions which are closely connected with dissatisfactions.

Under what kind of policy will the local education authority or the Head of the school allow the innovation to go forward? (Or, indeed, will there be a policy?) Will the teacher be on his own or will he be supervised? Will supervision, if it is there, be intended to make sure he makes no mistakes or to help him to resolve difficulties as he goes along? Will the added responsibility of doing something more arduous – even if, admittedly, more interesting – affect his salary? If he tries out something new will he be interpreted as doing this in order to please someone else? If so, will this prejudice well-established personal relationships with others in his school? In trying to estimate whether the range of satisfactions or of dissatisfactions carries the greater weight, the teacher will risk something like professional schizophrenia.

One way in which to simplify the dilemma of whether to adopt, or test, or reject, or at least think about curricular improvement is to take the view that the teacher is not simply an instructor; he will use his time and energies more economically if he regards himself as a manager of resources through which, or from which, others will learn.

How do teachers organise themselves?

In managing the resources which are essential for curriculum development time will have to be carefully used. One advocate of resource management (Ivor Davies, *The Management of Learning*, 1971) has categorised four broad functions for the teacher-manager:

- planning, or the establishment of objectives,
- organising, or the arranging of learning resources so as to achieve objectives effectively,
- leading, or motivating learners so that they achieve the objectives,
- controlling, or evaluating his own success in the other three tasks.

This, as another example of simplification, is still likely to pose confusing questions to those who have been trained mainly as instructors of one kind or another. The language of resources and of resource-management is still new, undeveloped and likely to be misleading unless it is firmly connected with the language of objectives. State what you are trying to achieve, establish what you need in order to achieve it, and work out the steps: it sounds simple, but to judge from a study by Philip Taylor (*How teachers plan their courses*, 1970) the task is either too strenuous or is regarded as too unimportant for teachers to do it very well.

Or it may be that the semantics of curriculum development have already produced a sense of boredom with the adjurations of philosophers, psychometrists and curriculum-builders about aims, objectives, evaluation and the rest of it. Tedium and resentment can slow things down as effectively as straight resistance. The manager of change must, again, avoid tedium: he must know the boredom-thresholds of those with whom he works.

Interest, stimulus and teachers' centres

The ways in which the wardens of teachers' centres are aware of the effects of boredom, of excessive requirements on teachers' spare time and of the degree to which a last straw of curricular demand may break the teacher's professional back, has already been touched on in the fifth chapter.

When teachers are 'over-coursed', the solution which most readily comes to the mind of anyone who runs a teachers' centre is to slacken off the demand, let teachers relax, let them be led back to some fresh interest in reform and curriculum development by methods which are not directly related to their day-to-day work.

There are both advocates and enemies in England and Wales of the policy of using teachers' centres as places which can have a social purpose as well as a training objective. For instance, how should one react to a half term programme of one small teachers' centre which features only three meetings? The first is a forum about educational visits and exchanges; the second is the explanation and discussion of a somewhat unique scheme produced by one school for a curriculum for the raising of the school leaving age; the third and last meeting of this part of the term is dedicated to the study of badgers.

Another centre dedicates a term's work to five meetings on local history, three discussions about a basic syllabus for primary mathematics, one meeting about the educational implications of dialect, another to deal with the maintenance of swimming pools, yet another about the teaching of swimming to younger pupils, three meetings given over to tuition and instrumental work in music for teachers, and finally one meeting to provide a forum for teachers of handicraft.

In addition to a programme of meetings, this latter centre also provides an area base for an LEA art loan scheme; it has provided, too, the beginnings of a record library. This same centre has made an analysis of its earlier work and has by analysing not only the content of meetings but also the number of attendances at each meeting provided itself with relatively full information upon which to base its future planning.

There are so many variations in the ways in which centres can serve their local teachers that it is difficult yet to attempt any assessment of the way in which one approach is more successful than another. One centre can retain some kind of following by making only very light demands upon its local people. Another can keep going only by providing a rich, quite highly professional and varied programme of sustained activity. Some centres provide a focus of interest which lies in the equipment and other resources which can be made available to teachers through the centres themselves. For instance, in a way comparable with the centre which acts as a base for art loans or for a record library, it is possible for an LEA to find outlets through centres for the loans of a School Museum Service.

Admittedly when teachers' centres spend a great deal of time in organising programmes of folk dancing or demonstrations of particular manufacturers' products in the teaching of art and craft, when much time is devoted to the teaching of guitar-playing to teachers, or when an interest in local history tends to dominate other professional activities, then one may justifiably doubt whether the centre is a proper avenue for curriculum development.

Usually a centre which has to appeal to its local teachers through a mixture of not very demanding professional courses and of rather more enticing social events is one which will be organised by a part-time secretary or warden. The full-time professional warden is more likely than his part-time colleague to want to prove himself and to want to prove to the teachers in his area that the centre is an appropriate and attractive place at which to work hard at the task of professional self-renewal.

But the seriousness of local effort will also be affected by the degree of expertness and readiness which the local authority gives in support of teachers who wish to attempt to change. The role of inspectors and advisers is crucial here.

Inspectors, advisers and the local management of change

The place of the central inspectorate (Her Majesty's Inspectors) has a long and notable history in the educational system of England and Wales. Although HMI were established well in advance of the establishment of local education authorities, the advisers and others employed by LEAs have no tradition of being in any form of tutelage to HMI. There is very little connection between the work of the two kinds of inspector; there has been practically no consultation until very recently about the ways in which national and local inspectors might work together or supplement one another's efforts. Comparably, the way in which HMI lend their weight to national courses of in-service training has little to do, again until recently, with the way in which local authorities deploy the services of advisers, inspectors and organisers to provide the bulk of such in-service training as is available to the average teacher in the English school.

It is unclear whether the distance which has historically existed between national and local inspectors could have been in any way narrowed and whether, if it had been narrowed, this would have produced any greater benefit to the process (or speed) of reform. Certainly HMI have throughout the greater part of the present century remained steadfast to their first duty of being independent arbiters of the quality of schools, of teaching and of teachers. They have admittedly lost their role of inspecting the attainment of children. Both teachers and LEAs are, however, still comparatively unclear as to whether HMI have, in fact, dropped their function of inspecting. It is insisted by the Department of Education and Science that HMI do not inspect LEAs; by implication this means that they inspect schools. However, since the mid-1960s it has been accepted that schools are no longer to be regularly *inspected* by HMI and there is even doubt whether any schools would within the next half decade be inspected at any time by those who work nationally.

This raises the question of whether HMI are employed in order to help schools or to help LEAs, or simply to act as informants of the Secretary of State for Education and Science about the quality of the system over which he or she presides at any one time. And even this definition of the function is one which would be difficult for either the Department or for the Inspectorate as an independent or quasi-independent corps d'élite to accept. When, for instance, in 1968 a former senior chief inspector gave evidence to a select committee of the House of Commons about the work and future of HMI, he complained that the relationship between the professional civil servant and Inspectors was bad. He, as the leader of the 400 or so members of the national inspectorate, was not accorded, so he said, status or access to Ministers comparable to that enjoyed, for instance, by Deputy

Under Secretaries of State. This complaint could hardly have been made had Her Majesty's Inspectors enjoyed a high status within the national Ministry.

If, however, they lack status nationally, what is their position locally? This, too, is becoming increasingly difficult to be precise about. HMI are certainly helpful to LEAs in the matter of preparing plans for reorganisation or in the submission of major building programmes year by year. They are helpful, too, in allowing LEAs to see themselves through other people's eyes – when an HMI, for instance, prepares snapshot reports about any particular aspect of an LEA's work.

When it comes to the management of curriculum change, the claim which HMI might make is that the bulk of their effort goes into the support of work which has been initiated by the Schools Council. Several examples – notably in mathematics, science and modern languages – can be pointed to as being areas of the curriculum where much of the pace for reform was set by senior members of HMI. There are certain legendary figures, such as Miss Edith Biggs, who have come to represent a movement of reform more or less entirely on their own. Behind these front runners there are, too, about 60 or 70 HMI who are working either directly for, or indirectly with, the Schools Council. They act as disseminators, field officers, specialists in certain sorts of consultancy, evaluators, or, simply, reporters.

But the traditional strength of HMI in the support of reform is both earlier than and unconnected with the Schools Council. HMI can sharpen other people's vision and can point to lessons of innovation which are not only interesting but which have also been tested. Principally, they can make it possible for things to be done at local level which might otherwise be hindered by national regulation. One example of facilitation in reform can be seen in in-service training.

It was not until 1971 that the first impact of HMI began to be felt in terms of systematic local renewal of curriculum. It was felt – and this will be described in more detail later – through the formulation of joint courses arranged by the DES and Area Training Organisations.

At the strictly local level of teachers' centres HMI are less often involved. They do, of course, contribute to single sessions and to short local courses. They are not, however, in constant contact with centres and they have no right of inspection. However, in seeing how some aspects of teacher education – notably those which are connected with the induction of new teachers – could be improved after the 1972 White Paper (*Education: A Framework for Expansion*), some HMI were notably imaginative and opportunistic in their support of local initiatives of innovation.

The lack of connection between the national inspectorate and local teachers' centres may have had its origins in a certain amount of distrust about the way in which teachers' centres were first encouraged. The Schools Council, after all, was acting independently of the Department of Education and Science. It was also acting independently of the Inspectors. This is in contrast to the way in which local advisers and inspectors had, from the beginning, been involved in the growth of local systems of curriculum development.

In some LEAs the establishment of teachers' centres was left entirely to the teachers and the formulation of programmes at those centres was a matter which was again laid so firmly at the teachers' door that the mistake may have been made of expecting too much too soon in terms of the teachers' professional self-awareness of their needs and capacities for retraining. In other LEAs teachers' centres have been regarded as vehicles through which inspectors and advisers may work. This, again, has had the disadvantage of bringing certain teachers to the point where they distrust the work of teachers' centres because they may after all be nothing other than yet another piece of the LEAs' mechanism for interfering with the schools' autonomy. But this admittedly is an extreme way of stating certain types of diffidence which are occasionally (but more rarely) expressed by teachers.

The most useful way in which local advisers and inspectors have assisted the growth of local curriculum development has probably been by taking up a position half way between two extremes. They have not assumed that teachers could venture on comparatively new ground without *any* assistance; nor have they truly accepted any sense of *right* in their own participation in local work. It is not by stealth that the local adviser or inspector reaches the point where he or she is trusted by the teacher. Rather, it is on the exercise of sensitivity, on a realistic sense of practical needs and practicable methods by which teachers may learn to meet their own needs that the good adviser can best base his efforts.

The fact that the participation of inspectors and advisers in local work differs very much from area to area is not surprising. There is no common training of advisers – and indeed there is basically no training at all of those who enter either national or local work in this field. There are, admittedly, professional conferences; there are national HMI courses to which advisers may occasionally be admitted; there are one or two LEAs who believe that the adviser is in as much need of in-service training as is the teacher himself. Basically, however, because of the lack of training, there are few common approaches, few common standards and few chances other than on the job, day by day, for local people to pool their experience of trying to provide the necessary support to teachers' centres. There is practically no literature on the subject and the only attempts which have been made to try to co-ordinate local work by sharing information has been through the setting-up of a handful of *ad hoc* conferences by the Schools Council itself.

Although the Schools Council and the Nuffield Foundation had, in their early days, set up (particularly in mathematics and in science) schemes by which advisers as well as a few administrators and a large number of teachers could be trained to train others, the pattern of training trainers or of advising advisers has not been sustained. Thus, if local curriculum development is to succeed with the help of advisers, it is up to the adviser himself to learn about the development and to make himself so familiar with new work that he is trusted by teachers. Then he has to take part in both the organisation and in the actual work of local development in such a way that he is treated by teachers as a genuine co-practitioner. All the new learners in curriculum development are equal – and they need to be.

Because the level of energy which an adviser can put into new work will differ from person to person, because of the empathy which he or she enjoys with teachers, because differences of intellectual and professional capacity obviously exist, the unevenness of quality in the support which is provided by advisers and inspectors is clearly understandable. Because of this it is understandable, too, why teachers will not take one uniform view of the participation of LEAs and their advisers in the teachers' own job of curriculum change. At this stage, the trustworthy, sound, hard-working and humane helper will be relied upon. But the adviser who still thinks in terms of inspection and of old-established statuses will be of little use.

There are in England and Wales about 2,500 local advisers and inspectors, then, together with about 400 HMI. There is little to be said about the present state of the participation of both types of inspectorate in local curriculum development work other than to say that less than what is possible seems to be achieved.

By 1974 local education authorities will have become larger and fewer. HMI will be fewer in number too; and it is, to say the least, unlikely that the number of LEA advisers will have increased very significantly. Where small local authorities will have come together to form larger unities it is inevitable that a new authority will have simply inherited those advisers and inspectors who were already at work in existing areas.

The rule has been that the smaller the authority, the fewer are its advisers. Thus where small authorities come together there will have been proportionately fewer advisers than where large counties joined with parts of other counties – or with large county boroughs who employed a sizeable number of advisers and inspectors.

There is room for improvement in the way in which full-time advisers and inspectors – those indeed who might be expected to play a very significant part in local development work – have so far worked. There is cause for concern that people who are experienced in causing educational change have little opportunity to take part in its actual management. They are, for instance, in a position to do far more than many of the wardens of teachers' centres. Local advisers, like HMI, are usually people with a broad experience of education, and, sometimes, with a notable reputation in their specialist field. By contrast the warden of a teachers' centre has come to his job anew. He need not necessarily have been acclaimed as a skilful practitioner nor even as anyone of very considerable experience in teaching or in administration. Usually the warden is employed, as we have seen, because he is energetic, because he is anxious to reform education – or because he has made a study of reform and of certain aspects in particular of curriculum and teaching method. However earnest they may be and however well-intentioned, wardens will be new in the game. Inexperience, freshness and vitality often go together. But newness can, too, be accompanied by a lack of wisdom and of insight.

We are, then, unclear at the moment whether enthusiasm and youth, theoretical knowledge and the wish to reform are in any way better forms of support – in human terms – for curriculum development than experience, wise interpretation of the past, a certain amount of caution about the acceptance of novelty, and considerable experience in working with and for the teachers. It is these latter qualities which are sometimes (but regrettably not always) possessed by advisers and inspectors. The time has yet to come when they will be fully deployed in the support of curriculum change.

Summary

This chapter has tried to draw together some of the issues which operate for and against local efforts of development. The ways in which wardens, inspectors, advisers, those who otherwise contribute to the work of teachers' centres (together with the teachers themselves) do their practical best in the cause of development is a patchwork of differing levels of experience, trust and success.

The teachers' centre is very much a creature of its locality. The amount of confidence which reposes in the warden is also a matter of local policy or, more likely, of local choice – and often the kind of choice which is neither systematic nor rational. The degree to which advisers are used to support the wardens and secretaries of centres varies almost whimsically. And the way in which HMI are not directly involved in local work raises questions about the future of the relationship of the national inspectorate with the work not only of teachers' centres and local advisers but with LEAs themselves. It will be

SUMMARY

some time yet before a clear answer can be found to those remaining problems which owe their origin to the history of tension between national and local inspection.

8 Curriculum development and teacher education

Until the publication of the James Report it was still regarded as comparatively progressive to emphasise that the education of teachers should have a great deal to do with coping with the continuous change to which education was bound to be subjected in the future. Change is accelerating, it was often claimed, and it was therefore necessary to shorten the gap between the introduction of novelty as a form of isolated experiment and the institutionalisation of an approved innovation within the curriculum of particular schools.

Until James there had been a certain amount of despair whether anything could be done about changing the initial training of teachers in such a way as to shake traditions which seemed basically to be related to a so-called grammar school way of doing things. The bulk of those who teach still in the colleges of education of England and Wales are, after all, teachers who came (three-quarters of them at least) from grammar schools seven or eight years before the publication of James. Their last experience, therefore, in the classroom was in the most stable part of the British system, the part where examination syllabuses and approved textbooks had had the greatest influence in preserving the past and in making it appear unnecessary to create change for the future.

Although it took a little time to find out whether any part of the James Report should be implemented, and although crudity and oversimplification of the Report's ideas took their toll before the publication of the 1972 White Paper, nevertheless teacher education can never be quite the same again. It has been placed on official record that there is urgent need for the teaching profession to reappraise its efforts and to renew the educational process. To regard this as a continuing professional responsibility is now an unavoidable obligation.

We can expect early answers to questions about the readiness with which those who control the initial education of teachers will respond to the need to take curriculum development seriously. Will they now do something for the preparation of students in this field apart from a short exposure to the specialisms and enthusiasm of one or two lecturers or heads of department within a college?

While it will have taken time for the James Report to work its way into action, the world of in-service education will have altered too. The Report, after all, put forward the notion that the school should be responsible for the up-dating and retraining of its own teachers. The difficulty of this idea lies partly in the risk that a school may be a mediocre institution with teachers of a uniformly mediocre quality. They keep the ship afloat and they keep it pointing more or less in one direction – but it moves with no great sense of momentum and with little thrust. The school stays out of trouble but retains some reputation for stability – but no stimulus need exist for a teacher to change his or her way of doing things.

This is a problem which may, one hopes, be theoretical. We still know only little about resources that will be needed for a James-type of programme of continuous education (once the student has completed his formal accreditation) to become widely available – and even then the full scheme is not expected to be in action before 1982. We do, however, know that the recommendations of the White Paper for the continuous training of teachers is set against a background of very marked change in the pattern of in-service training over the past decade – and that this, in turn, reflects very clearly the movement of curriculum reform.

Even as late as the mid-1960s the guesses and well-informed estimates which could be made about the volume of teacher participation in in-service training revealed pessimistically low figures. One guess was as low as 3% in 1965; a more optimistic estimate put it at 12%. However, by 1968–9 the percentage was shown, in the first full survey carried out by the Department of Education and Science, to be as high as something between 35% and 45%. A period of less than a decade had, thus, seen a very considerable growth in emphasis on in-service training. It had seen, too, a number of successful efforts to create more productive connections between separate institutions which have responsibility for such training. Most important, it had seen in-service training become accepted as something which teachers needed and expected.

This was a long way from the days when the National Union of Teachers alone of the major teachers' associations organised two or three day refresher courses every two years or so in each area of the country. Those refresher courses still continue: if they grow dim in contrast to the more brightly illuminated novelties of other kinds of in-service training, they still hold a worthy and unique place in the history of teachers' professional retraining. The question is how far we can continue to use any of the traditional mechanism of in-service training in order to assist the process of curriculum development. Training is decidedly an important part of the mechanism: those who manage change must know how the thing works. But the only picture which can be accurately drawn is one which depicts how in-service training *now* assists in the management of development.

Present forms of in-service training

In contrast to courses, conferences, seminars and workshops, the broadest definition of in-service training would include all informal and accidental effects on a teacher's work. The sum of informal effects may amount to very much the same thing as those of formal courses but since one can scarcely account in a rational way for the impact of influences which are arbitrary and highly variable (television, popular journals, chance meetings and conversations) any analysis of the retraining of teachers is more safely confined to its formal aspects. What has, then, to be left out is the process of self-training which comes from a teacher's perception of connections between his informal reading (or listening or TV viewing) and his professional work.

The assistant teacher is, with the Head, the principal agent of change in the curriculum within any school: this is the assumption on which national, regional and local policies of curriculum development are based. National curriculum projects, once they have passed out of the experimental stage, depend for their dissemination on the arrangement of a number of teachers' instructional courses at various centres. These courses are, during the first round, intended to familiarise a handful of people from any one local education authority in a new project's work: subsequent courses help this handful to familiarise a larger number of advisers, teachers and others within the same education authority area. These courses are set up by the Schools Council and, sometimes jointly, by the Nuffield Foundation. They are helped by the Department of Education and Science.

Below national level, courses of training are often mounted by the Schools Council jointly with a university Institute of Education in the locality of its own Area Training Organisation. An Area Training Organisation (ATO) includes all the local education authorities within a university Institute of Education's area; the local education authorities, the colleges of education which fall under the aegis of the Institute as well as the Institute's own professional staff contribute, usually jointly, to the in-service training programme of the ATO. At local level, local education authorities themselves are the sponsors of in-service training with or without help from Schools Council project staff, or Her Majesty's Inspectors, or members of the staff of the local Institute of Education. And local authorities are, throughout all other changes, the largest providers of in-service training in England and Wales.

The attendance of teachers at national and regional courses which are connected with development projects tends to be by invitation. This means that teachers are usually hand-picked. This in itself gives an air of prestige to this kind of training. Also, the first corps of teachers in training schemes of this kind is expected to be able to train others. Again, the local education authority who sends teachers to courses within this category needs the teacher's help and is prepared to pay. All official expenses are met. This is not usual with, for instance, local courses where the teacher has his travel expenses paid but where he is often expected to pay a substantial part of the cost of his subsistence. Unlike local courses, too, those at national and regional level have an element of competition about them; these are often well-attended because authorities nominate or invite specific teachers to attend. Strictly local courses are more often open to volunteers: anyone can take part who is interested, who is accepted for a course, and who has the time to attend it.

Between national dissemination courses which are already connected with curriculum development and the local come-as-you-please course, several variants exist. First, national HMI courses on subjects, subject areas or 'age-phases' of pupils can do something to prepare the ground for curriculum change. Among the most important of these are those run by a group of HMI whose concern it is to retrain the Heads of secondary schools in school organisation – in terms of social, curricular and disciplinary control as well as in the use of resources.

At local level a second and comparatively new type of course is the joint responsibility of the ATOs and of the Department of Education and Science through HMI. The DES puts money into these courses and local education authorities enjoy the benefit of highly structured and continuous (40-session) courses on concentrated themes. The conditions on which these are provided are varied: for instance the ATO and HMI can arrange for two or three major injections of training (in the shape of residential weekends) at the beginning, middle and end of a long course. Between the residential periods, weekly or fortnightly afternoon-plus-evening sessions would be held at centres which are suitably accessible to teachers. For these intermediate sessions the ATO would find leaders, organisers and outside speakers. This type of package means that education authorities have to move away from the idea of a concentrated course being attended by a widely scattered number of separate teachers: local groups have to be organised who can give one another support in the continued training which goes on between the dates of residential courses. Also, the range and type of course is limited: the choice is made on the basis of, particularly, the usefulness which teachers in certain areas may be expected to find in them. In other words the joint use of regional (ATO) and national (DES/HMI) resources is intended to meet local needs in as systematic, rich and controlled a manner as possible.

If these joint national-cum-regional courses are properly organised, they appear likely to bring very considerable benefit to the process of curriculum development. To be properly organised they have to be concerned with themes of pressing and continuous significance; they have to be less concerned with methods of *teaching* than with problems which are part of education's fabric, whether it is new content and new method or the attitude towards (and acceptability of) new ideas which seem principally to be at stake at any one moment. Thus, the courses must be few in number, because this ensures that only significant themes *can* be chosen and because it will not make excessive demands on teachers' energies. Nor will it make excessive demands on the capacity of local education authorities to release teachers in paid time. It also means that choices of subject have to be made which really matter to those regional interests which are represented in an ATO. In the 1970s a certainty about some themes seems unavoidable: secondary school reorganisation, the extension of educational facilities to those children who used to be regarded as severely subnormal and ineducable, the exploration of methods by which educational experience can be given to pre-school children within an expanding national policy for the extension of nursery education, the detailed examination of how the linguistic needs of young children in their first years at school can be met – in different ways from region to region, each of these has relevance to growth and development in curriculum.

Each topic such as these requires some degree of specialised local treatment and each meets, it is hoped, the expressed needs of teachers. Further, while training time is limited and while it is a matter almost exclusively of voluntary effort on the part of teachers, the way in which resources for innovation can be most beneficially used is more likely to be found by concentrating energy and attention on a narrow range of topics. When the teacher's sabbatical term (whether in every seventh or fifth year) for training or for some other method of professional refreshment becomes a reality, the approach to in-service training can afford to be different.

Continuous training: teachers' associations

Other types of course which feed the need for teachers' preparation in the area of curriculum change are provided by subject associations and by teachers' professional associations. In the first category the most successful associations in England so far have been the Association of Science Education, the National Association for the Teaching of English and a small group of associations which centre their interests on school mathematics. In each of these a marked awareness has been visible from the mid-1960s and earlier about the challenge of curriculum reform. Other associations dealing, for instance, with geography, history and classics have responded more slowly – but they have nevertheless rallied. These have answered (and not simply in a style of resistant self-defence) expectations of change which have been expressed for their subjects by sundry development projects of the Schools Council and Nuffield Foundation. And in mathematics and English, the associations have themselves initiated important development work on a national scale, sometimes with – but more often without – the support of public funds.

The professional associations (and the National Union of Teachers more noticeably than others) have, as we have seen, some tradition of providing refresher courses. In such courses a wide range of topics is covered, usually in lecture form by an outside speaker. The choice of topic depends upon what is demanded by teachers and upon what is in vogue. The value of this type of course can be belittled, often because little or no work in preparation or follow-up is required of the teachers. A two day shot-in-the-arm is expected to be enough. But it clearly cannot be enough. Nevertheless, on the margin there have to be included two considerable reckonings of benefit. First, most local education authorities automatically give paid leave of absence for NUT refresher courses: schools may be closed, but little hint of disruption is ever heard of from LEAs, from parents or from teachers. Secondly, the teachers' association refresher course – in a manner which will not always apply to, say, LEA single-topic courses – encourages teachers of a *variety* of levels of enthusiasm, learnedness or conscientiousness to come together. It may be regarded as a social meeting or as an earnestly professional one; but however it is approached and even if it *is* for only two days in a year, a large number of teachers can come together in order to improve their capacity as educators. Whether courses succeed or fail in bringing about an improvement, the expectation that they should do so is itself enough to achieve a great deal for professional morale.

Continuous training: local education authorities

About the local course, which has been described as come-as-you-please, something more needs to be said; local education authorities with a substantial number of specialist advisers have increasingly used these officers for in-service training. Just as the by now common local change in title from 'Inspector' to 'Adviser' has meant something to education in general and to curriculum in particular, so the overt movement from inspection to the *guidance* of teachers has placed on authorities an onus to provide the retraining which teachers need.

At its worst in-service training is provided in response to a random pattern of local requests: these are not always likely to match professional need. The LEA has to decide whether to imply that it knows better than the teacher in providing courses – and knowing better here means no more than exercising a type of synoptic foresight which enables an authority to satisfy itself when it looks at the near or middle future. If its policies are going to require particular skills, attitudes or sympathies from its teachers, an LEA is entitled to provide courses which will elicit change. Comprehensive school reorganisation, early school deprivation, the establishment of middle schools and work connected with an older leaving age are just four of the most common challenges for which many LEAs have in recent years felt that they should prepare their serving teachers.

That an LEA should use planning and some degree of foresight as a basis for its future programme of in-service training courses seems natural. However, the basis is sometimes one which seems to be defined entirely by the preferences or practices of its separate advisers. Because certain types of course in, say, physical education or science are said always to have been provided, and because they have been liked by specialist teachers who have the comfort year after year of knowing what to expect, it goes without saying that this is no reason for creating any kind of *policy* around what is simply a comfortable tradition.

A middle path, however, between the proper meeting of teachers' needs and the giving of free rein to individual advisers' preferences is difficult to steer. For how, after all, is a local authority to know what its teachers do need? If questionnaire and quasi-formal enquiries are used, it is unsurprising that teachers should not want to reveal themselves as needing new information about traditional topics or that they should be diffident about associating themselves with demands for courses about what is new.

No local authority, any more than an Institute of Education, or HMI, or a teachers' association wants to provide courses which are not going to be supported. No one, either, wants to provide something so *avant garde* that it will not be understood. Much depends for the success both of in-service training policies as a whole and of particular courses on the choice of individual popularisers and interpreters. In-service training in the end depends upon the credibility and attractiveness of whoever it is who plays the central role in a particular course.

Forms of training

In-service training provided by local education authorities can take several different forms. A weekend course ($2\frac{1}{2}$ days), a working-week course ($4\frac{1}{2}$ days), a one term course (12 weekly sessions, evening and late afternoon), a two term course (12 *double* weekly sessions spread over the second half of one term and the first half of the following term, with the holiday period deliberately left for additional reading and with each double session entailing, first an absence from some part of the teachers' work and, secondly, entailing a willingness on the part of the teacher to give up his own evening hours to

FORMS OF TRAINING

in-service training) – these and other styles of training are common enough to let it be expected that authorities should have more or less shared policies.

In 1969 Brian Cane published for the National Foundation for Educational Research a survey of the practices of three authorities in providing in-service training (NFER, Occasional Publications Series No. 22, *In-service training*). He revealed disparities in the degree of attractiveness which programmes held for teachers, he revealed differing policies of financial assistance for teachers and showed, too, a wide discrepancy between the types of courses which were offered. A more detailed survey carried out by H.E.R. Townsend for the Department of Education and Science published in 1970 (Statistics of Education, Special Series No. 2: *Survey of in-service training of teachers*) showed the in-service training that teachers were getting in the late 1960s in contrast to what they actually wanted. This, together with Cane's survey, enabled a good composite picture to be built up of the degree to which teachers felt themselves to be properly catered for in terms of retraining for, particularly, curriculum development.

Earlier in 1968 the publication, in preparation of the raising of the school leaving age, of *Enquiry 1* had included a range of teachers' responses to questions about the kind of training they felt they needed for this one major change in educational policy. The first need was for courses on new developments in particular subjects and on new techniques for putting subjects over to pupils; second in priority, teachers wanted discussions and conferences with other teachers in order to help them to pool their experiences and problems. Then came a wish to become familiar with work in different fields of employment. Finally came the desire for courses in social science about the backgrounds and behavioural problems of fifteen year old leavers.

These wishes differed in several ways from those which are described in the Townsend survey; the one represented the results of a survey which was linked to a particular problem. The other took a bird's eye view of the whole field.

The idea of in-service training as something which can, and which teachers allow, to shape curriculum is relatively complex. A number of agencies are at work in the field but the nearest that retraining has yet come to having a strategy within which teachers' wants, local authority needs, the training capacity of a region and joint planning can have substantial effect is within the idea of combined efforts of HMI and the ATOs.

However, another combination of effort which could be equally valuable, namely between those in colleges of education who give initial training to teachers and who are in a good position to contribute very significantly to later retraining, this has taken time to find its pattern. Early attempts at local work lacked co-ordination – even within a single region. Until the 1972

White Paper there could certainly have been no national framework. By now, however, the need for colleges of education to diversify their provision, to take up a new role in teacher-induction and in the continuous training of serving teachers – as well as to accept a broader task within the field of Higher Education as a whole – each of these demands sharpens the contribution which colleges will make.

Training for management

Year by year, in-service training which is connected with separate subjects or with separate curriculum projects shows signs of growing in strength. In such courses, however, little is done about the organisation of change and little seems to be done in terms of training new teachers to show that education in any of its aspects requires management.

In the education of teachers the school appears to be described as a single whole only in its *social* dimensions; very seldom it is described in terms of organisation or management. This could be because the job of a Head, or deputy Head or of any other senior teacher who has some undefined authority is too difficult or too unknown to talk about. And this in turn could be the way in which the power of Heads and others is reinforced to the point, for instance, that the NUT is worried about the independence of assistant staffs.

Courses arranged by HMI, Institutes of Education and LEAs do much to help a few Heads and a limited number of assistant teachers to prepare for school reorganisation at both the primary and the secondary level. What is, however, wrong is that still too few are affected by these courses.

What on the other hand is optimistic is that those courses on these lines which do exist take a large view of school organisation and examine the interplay between the design of curriculum and the formulation of timetables, the appointment and disposition of teaching staff and the balance which they are intended to hold within the curriculum. These courses, too, enable teachers to see both that there is an interdependence between resources and pedagogic decisions and that there are different ways of reaching decisions. Some of the approaches to this kind of training stress the quantifiable elements of management; decision-making is the central task and the range of decisions in any one school is limited by what is measurable in terms of accommodation, staffing, equipment and the number of pupils. When the limits are known within which a decision can be made, the quality of the decision then receives attention.

One form of training for secondary school Heads is arranged by a small group of HMI. These have come to be known by the initials of the original group who organised the courses – the Committee on the Staffing,

Management and Organisation of Schools, COSMOS. Their concern is principally with the kinds of decision which a Head or a deputy must make in respect of staff, time and building. Basically the courses are intended to train people in new ways of making decisions about the disposition of conventional resources; at a time of change the Head has still to work within the limits of traditional timetables, staffrooms and classrooms. The approach of the COSMOS-type of course pays particular attention to the relationship between curriculum and time. Curriculum analysis is a skill for which Heads need training; if they acquire the skill they can see through the confusing mass of information which is held within the conventional timetable. The timetable is something about which teachers can tell anecdotes. It is difficult for one school to describe its organisation to another school and in this particular task of communication the timetable should be, but is not, a useful form of illustration. Timetables are built up – sometimes over generations; the accretions of habit which are contained in them are difficult to understand and to justify. They tell an unclear story.

The need to go beyond the timetable and to find another way of describing the relationship between a school's purposes, its curriculum and the way in which it uses its building and its teachers – this has presented a particular challenge for COSMOS courses. Work by T. I. Davies, W. M. White and others in devising a notation in which to carry out the analysis of curriculum has enabled Heads and senior staff to compare those differing approaches to curriculum planning which are adopted by different schools. To some Heads it has revealed that their own school's curriculum is based on assumptions and little more. It has, for others, revealed how faithfully the allocation of time to certain activities reflects the importance which they would ideally like to attach to those activities. Thus, schools where Heads have felt secure in their wish (and in their plan) to devote more time and staff to the needs, for instance, of slow learners in the second and third year are sometimes revealed as failing. Instead of the second and third year it is the sixth and seventh year which receives special attention. And more staff time is allocated, perhaps, to the high achievers than to the low achievers.

In having a way of actually knowing whether he is achieving what he hopes to do in terms of distributing resources, the Head who has attended an organisation and management course mounted by HMI will derive a particular benefit. It will not always be comfortable to have such new knowledge but, once given it, the Head is bound to remain aware of the kind of distortion which a curriculum (and a timetable) may suffer unless the large view of his school's management is kept constantly in view. He will be aware of how much bonus time and staff skill he has in hand – for every secondary school does have sufficient room for manoeuvre for choices of emphasis to be possible. He will be aware, too, of the limits within which he has to work if he wishes to organise his school's curriculum differently.

The deceptively simple and practical approach of COSMOS courses carries considerable advantage; it reassures Heads at a time of uncertainty that they are, after all, only dealing with old problems in a new way. When they return to their schools they go back with messages which are concerned with conventional problems and with different but straightforward solutions. When passed on to other members of staff this is intended to help them to understand the way in which novelty is to be cast within their particular school.

The effect of management courses of the practical type will be felt only slowly on secondary schools; what is regrettable is that comparable courses for Heads of primary schools scarcely yet exist. Apart from some pioneering work by ILEA and some sporadic activity in a few Institutes, HMI courses and LEA courses, nothing is offered to encourage those who are responsible for primary schools to gain any new awareness about the special types of curricular problem which are bound to affect schools where teachers are mainly concerned with general subjects and not with specialisation. Admittedly, the current concern in many LEAs with the setting up and organisation of middle schools has led to a large number of short and mid-term courses of training in devising a new 8–12 or 9–13 curriculum. There are also courses which deal not only with curriculum design for the middle years but also with school organisation. In time these may affect, tangentially at least, the way in which some Heads look at their way of running the conventional primary school. But until in-service training in primary school management becomes more widespread, the proper assimilation of curriculum novelty into the mainstream of primary school activity will be delayed. And if it is the larger primary school which is more rigid than the small unit in its capacity for change, it is the large school at which, because problems of organisation multiply, the management of curriculum change will become increasingly difficult.

Not directly related to the particular needs of either primary or secondary schools and yet providing useful experience for administrators both inside and outside schools, some larger and longer courses of management training are arranged along lines which take greater account of the place of the social sciences in education. Typical amongst these is the long course which is designed (for senior administrators as well as Heads and others) by, for instance, the University of London's Institute of Education under the direction of Dr George Baron. Emphasis is given here not only to dissertation and the discussion of what has been practically observed in schools and elsewhere but also to an examination of the interplay between sociology and politics and to the way in which the larger issues which surround any public enterprise make a direct or indirect effect upon the day-to-day conduct of education. Those who attend this kind of course are likely to feel that they have witnessed a demonstration of the large pattern into which public education fits. Whether or not they return to a school or to an education office with any sense of having a nostrum which can effect a quick remedy is doubtful. Nevertheless this larger, slightly more abstract and somewhat more detached kind of training has considerable value. The only regret is that it can only provide for very few people in any one year.

For those whose work lies not so much within schools as within the sector of Further Education the work of the Further Education Staff College at Coombe Lodge, Blagdon, provides a longer series of courses. Here it is possible for Principals, vice-principals, heads of department and other senior members of college staff to attend a series of weekly or fortnightly courses which provide a continuous pattern of management training. Because the arrangement is that somebody can attend for a fortnight, then go away to digest what has been learned over months of the resumption of normal work in a college, and can then return (and perhaps for a third time) – all this allows the participant to learn by application, to learn by the capacity to take back problems to which fresh attention has been drawn and to learn by asking questions about the complex nature of problems which he has perhaps not hitherto fully seen. It is quite clear that the staff college approach has a great deal to offer to those in further education. It may be idealistic, extravagant or unreal to hope that this idea could be extended to cover the continued management training of those who run British schools; nevertheless the attempt should be made to distil a few lessons from which a larger number of people can draw benefit.

The three types of course which have already been described have a very heavy emphasis on the management of change – and change is in each case viewed as a matter of organisation. In contrast there are those types of management training which pay more attention to the psychological and socio-psychological nature of organisations and of the processes of adaptation through which they pass.

Courses of this latter kind are provided by the Tavistock Institute for Human Relations, by the Grubb Institute, and by the Advisory Centre for Education or by the Careers Research Advisory Centre at Cambridge. The bulk of training comes from people who are well experienced both in the practicalities of education and in the perception and analysis of those social and personal events which accompany change.

There are signs of interest in this kind of approach to the personal aspects of management in the work of several institutes of Education. For instance, at the University Department of Education in Bristol, the studies of Elizabeth Richardson under the aegis of the Schools Council have over several years now taken a long look at the organisation of change in one large comprehensive school in an area near to Bristol. The research has involved much questioning; questioning in itself is its own kind of training.

In each type of management training, the way in which change is looked at is coloured by the extent to which those who are responsible for it view education as a fixed institution or as a process. There are fairly complex arguments within the sociology of education for preferring one view to the other. Here, however, it is enough to say that both the institutional and the 'process-oriented' views can teach serving Heads and administrators much that they have not previously known. In particular, lessons have to be learned about the variety of resources upon which change depends.

Training in the use of resources

It is not particularly helpful to remind those who manage change that their resources include the willingness of people, human capacities, predilections and whims as well as books, equipment, accommodation, money for educational visits, new expertness in the form of those who can handle certain types of new resource material, or some fresh willingness to create and use materials which are unconventional to the teacher. Nevertheless, the range of resources *is* broad and the degree to which anyone who is responsible for managing change can accustom himself, early on, to a new realisation of what it is that can help him is considerably aided in the smooth management of novelty.

One example of resource which cannot too easily, nor too obviously, be taken into account is the degree of self-awareness which a teacher can bring to innovation. Few of us take easily to change; indeed, acceptance may sometimes be taken as an indication of gullibility – or of something uncritical in the human make-up. Basically, however, if people have a capacity to think and to act clearly, there is a better chance that innovation will be handled with seriousness and efficiency. To promote self-awareness is not, however, easy. The direct exhortation of teachers to think harder or to puzzle out their objectives with greater assiduity is an approach which has already been proved by its crudity (and by the risks which it carries of being patronising) to be ineffective. If a teacher is to look afresh at his professionalism and to see how his present approach might help – or fit in – with what is new, he has to see himself through the eyes of no one other than himself.

Models and micro-teaching

One very literal way in which certain aspects of a teacher's professional performance can be seen anew is through the filming or video-taping of classroom behaviour. Much has been claimed for this kind of self-perception after experiments in the United States. The approach may seem over-simple; what, after all, are we to expect merely from the visible aspects of a teacher's performance? Are factors such as integrity, personality, forcefulness, and commitment not likely to matter more? If they do matter more and if, as more or less spiritual qualities, they are likely to elude visibility, is the outward and visible style of a teacher's performance at all significant? The answer has to be that what is visible is, certainly, significant. We do, after all, expect qualities such as sincerity and commitment to show through in any human activity. Conversely, insincerity or apathy or prejudice or a hostile personal attitude in a relationship which should be completely professional is not only visible but also disturbing.

There may, then, be profound and disconcerting implications for the teacher who can view himself in his ordinary contact with pupils and who can mull over what has been recorded. Is he, as a result, to express (to himself) approval or disapproval of his way of doing things? Is he to admit that overt classroom behaviour – a gesture, the degree to which a teacher smiles, the way in which he or she responds to ordinary routine contact from minute to minute with pupils – that this is in the end the very stuff upon which teaching and learning is based?

In the context of teaching in England and Wales he is bound to admit that the practical, pragmatic, real situation of *this* teacher with *these* pupils amounts to much more than a great deal of thinking. And if the teacher is involved in curriculum innovation, if he or she has been subjected, during in-service training, to a bombardment of theory about the handling of change actually within the classroom – a rare experience at the present stage of training, one would suspect – the effect of self-observation will inevitably (even if grudgingly) be acknowledged as salutary.

Whatever the teacher's intentions may be, however profound the thought which has been given to what is being taught, however much it may be hoped that there is less dependence in any particular classroom on the teacher (and more dependence upon the learner), this goes out of the window if the living performance which the teacher puts up in front of pupils and students is one which is at variance with his or her professed ideal.

To arrange for teachers to see their own performances in professional terms is, then, straightforward. It is technically possible. It is helpful – and it may sometimes be threatening. As a part of training in the management of resources it is something which ought to be encouraged by Heads and by others. But anyone who advocates this has, immediately, to add the rider that recorded self-observation ought to be a matter which is very private to the teacher himself. There ought to be no compulsion (if video-taping of classroom behaviour can be arranged) for anyone other than the teacher himself or herself to be involved in reviewing what has happened. This is a simple matter of human justice; to see oneself at work may be sufficiently disturbing, quite often, for very few morals to have to be pointed and for few messages to have to be underlined. If you surprise or shock yourself by your own mirrored performance, then you are likely to correct yourself very quickly indeed. If, however, you are still numbered amongst those who do not agree that the camera never lies, you will rationalise and argue that the observed performance – as recorded – is not the real you. In that circumstance, immovable resistance and insensitivity begins to become a problem.

The remedial nature of this kind of micro-teaching is, of course, only a beginning. The teacher who can see that his gesticulative and other overtly discernible styles of behaviour are unfitting to the projection of a new idea is bound to learn some lessons fairly quickly: a very obvious style of resource can be freshened up and viewed anew, quickly and easily.

Although it is more than ten years old, the process of recording a teacher's performance – and of playing it back to him – has not yet become very highly refined. For instance, the shape of the exercise has so far remained more or less the same in each experiment: the teacher and the critic (usually a more experienced teacher – on the lines of the original experiment at the University of Stanford), have, together, reviewed a video-tape. The less experienced teacher has then gone through a 're-teach'. This second attempt may have short term purposes which are connected simply with practising some straight skills of organising a lesson; alternatively, the purposes of review and of rethinking have sometimes had a more distant perspective. The teacher may see the business of classroom behaviour in the context of a strategy rather than, simply, of daily tactics.

If this longer view is sought, the teacher and the experienced practitioner who offers a critique of his first effort will, together, be interested in something other than the more obvious skills. Three other elements can come into play: the setting-up of a teacher's work and the facilities with which he works, the participants in the interplay of teacher and taught and the programme, plan, or outline within which the work is to be done – these are parts of the overall transaction. The degree to which a teacher can learn something about these three elements from micro-teaching depends largely, perhaps, on the extent to which he can believe in (and use) models.

If I watch an expert doing the job which I myself hope to perform, I inevitably shape my professional conduct on what I see – if, that is, I am still at the stage of being teachable. If I have a good and credible model, imitation alone may accelerate my process of learning something new. But on the other hand, the model by itself may not be a sufficient stimulus.

Because of this the teacher, in his own learning, is in much the same condition as his pupils. His dilemma is that of wondering whether those

MODELS AND MICRO-TEACHING

whom he teaches can learn from an untreated experience as much as they might extract from something constructed, contrived and made-up. The dilemma in micro-teaching is that of whether the teacher can bear to look at his whole performance with the voice of the critic in his ear, pointing out what is good, bad, usable or useless. Or should he look at himself only in an edited process – with only those parts of his performance left in view which are useful in indicating good (or bad) morals?

In micro-teaching, then, the teacher has the chance to view his own classroom behaviour and to draw morals. He may, alternatively, watch his own behaviour alongside that of a model master-teacher – again, with or without a commentary. Or he can, without any implied comparison, simply be exposed to the demonstration of a master-teacher's own conduct. The less experienced practitioner is then left with the open question of whether to learn or not to learn, or (more crudely) to imitate or not to imitate.

The implication of using a model, when we view this in connection with the large business of curriculum reform, may be more important for the prospects of success in the movement of change as a whole than in the attempt to alter an individual teacher's classroom behaviour. We might, too, suspect that a model is likely to be imitated wholeheartedly only if some part of what is either practised or preached has previously and independently been accepted as a significant novelty. In other words, the first stimulus to change can quite likely be something other than a good model. But a good model reinforces and amplifies the message.

Another implication of micro-teaching stems from the tendency for it to open up questions about facilities and the setting for a teacher's work, about those who participate in the interplay of teacher and taught and about the place in which everything is conducted. Some of these questions are part of the social scene of teaching, others belong to the physical scene. And in one very obvious way, the use of models and the observation of the work or ideas of other people here creates a special problem.

It has been customary for many years for Heads and others to arrange for their assistant staff to visit other schools and to see other teachers at work. This is never totally satisfactory because no one can watch somebody else at work without altering the circumstances in which that work is done. And just as direct classroom or lecture room observation is seldom very productive, so the straight replication of ideas, social relationships or physical conditions must often fail.

If, however, it is claimed that it is not the observation of other teachers but, instead, the perception of how they view their work, plan it, create the right atmosphere, organise resources – that it is these things which matter, then it connects with the straightforward approach which is already adopted in some teachers' centres. Teachers' centres, however, are not likely to be good at dealing with the physical setting in which teaching takes place. Teachers can, if they still need to, learn about the arrangement and rearrangement of furniture in a classroom. But they cannot alter the shape of a room nor the way in which spaces in a school give help in, for instance, making the access to resources for learning easier. Often, because they can do nothing about the shape, size and juxtaposition of rooms, teachers feel frustration. They are likely, in this mood, to say that they would take innovation seriously if they had the right physical conditions to work in. And there are people other than teachers themselves who are responsible for physical conditions.

The physical setting

It is easy to overlook or to ignore the impact of those whose job it is to design the physical facilities of schools. It is, for instance, now many years since secondary schools were planned with, for instance, one simple rectangular area which was described as a library. It is many years, too, since the disappearance of the idea that only the *secondary* school should have a purpose-built library. Most local education authorities have, for example, moved over to the kind of thought which dictates that all infant rooms should have a book corner and that all junior pupils' rooms should have either open access library shelves or a generally labelled resource area into which children might move freely as their need for particular reference work dictates.

Although a certain amount of obscurity has grown up around the design of buildings, the development of ideas about how the use of a space connects with its design is simple. In the early 1960s it had become (largely through the work of David Medd) a matter of conventional wisdom in secondary schools for subject rooms to be grouped in such a way that an additional area could be 'won' so as to provide a particular resource area which comprised, perhaps, book space or a map space or, in a more sophisticated way, a facility for viewing filmstrips or for listening to tapes. In this field, much of the thinking in England had derived from North American experience once the tradition of library halls had there been discarded. Multi-resource areas, places where people could come and go freely, where need rather than the timetable dictated how easily someone should be able – in terms of individualised learning – to turn to a particular type of resource, all this has become part of the design of British schools. It has not so readily been something which we can properly afford; the cost limits of British schools make it difficult to provide the same degree of flexibility as is found in many North American schools. However, a beginning has been made; the difficulty is largely now one not so much of providing spaces for resource areas as of determining exactly what it is that a resource area should do. And purpose and function is difficult to pin down too firmly.

The brief to which an architect of a school will work is customarily drawn up by someone on the administrative side of a local education authority. The writer of an architect's brief may be a full-time administrator or an adviser. Over the years certain conventions of modernity have been established. Some of these have their origins in building bulletins from the Department of Education and Science and in the work of that department's Architects and Building Branch. Other ideas, particularly for the equipment and design of specialist rooms in secondary schools, come from enlightened individuals or from pressure groups within teachers' associations. Notably, the design of home economics rooms and of certain types of science laboratory has owed almost as much to teachers' interest as to advice from the Department of Education and Science.

Nevertheless, although the design of British schools achieves great feats of flexibility and ingenuity within continually tight cost limits, there are difficulties. For instance, it is relatively easy to say that adolescents should be allowed free access to specialist reference centres which are connected with subject teaching spaces; they should also have access to general library areas. But how are the functions of subject areas and of general libraries to be defined and separated? This difficulty in one sense is of the same nature as that of determining how far a secondary school child should be allowed to follow his own bent rather than be led by the person who is teaching him. And the question has to find an answer which is satisfying in a variety of ways. When are pupils to be left to themselves? When and how must they be controlled in their learning?

The moment and the method of treating learners in either a free or a structured way depends on both the physical and the human ambience.

Anything that happens between people has to happen in a place. Studies which are concerned with the way in which places can affect people look upon basic space as a mere container. Within that container (the room, the hall, the library, the gymnasium), the nature of what happens can be modified more or less at will. Furnishing, lighting, relative humidity, smell and temperature – each of these can alter the bare physical setting. But so also can the duration and manner of what happens as well as what leads up to it and follows.

To repeat this kind of simple statement is, in one way, merely to say what is obvious to every teacher. But what is less obvious is the degree to which teachers themselves feel responsible for the way in which the setting for their work can be modified. And if this is followed further, the question might be asked of whether the simple physical design of a school is after all the most unalterable part of the scene.

Whether, then, we think in terms of resources and their physical handling or of their accessibility and use, the shape of a space is, in the end, less important than the way in which the teacher organises things *in* that space. And, so that the argument may come back in its circle, this is where concerns about method – of the kind which are highlighted by microteaching – are common to the total process of managing what is new. The physical aspect (whether it be a teacher's gesture, the look on his face, the warmth of the classroom or the glare of the sun through a window) is more important than we sometimes admit. But behind what is physical must lie planning, thought and the awareness of exactly what is going on.

Individualisation of learning

We are already accustomed in the design of new schools and in the extensions of old schools to assume that children are taught for a part of the time – and that the physical environment of learning should be one which provides for a mixture of opportunities. It is easier to arrange for this variety within primary education than it is at the secondary stage. Teachers in primary schools are by now accustomed to the idea of children moving more freely about a conglomeration of classrooms and within and around collections of books, materials and other sources of information and assistance.

In secondary schools the tradition of class teaching survives more strongly. This is in part a result of the design of schools; teaching boxes are there and children will remain within them. In front of each group of children the main source of learning will be the teacher who directs operations. In order to move away from class teaching and the implicit idea of instruction, secondary school teachers have to be re-educated to the idea of child-based learning and they also have to be led to the use of such new buildings as they may occasionally have the benefit of. This brings into question the degree to which the secondary school teacher is prepared to *diminish* his role as the *leader* of his children's learning. It also brings into question what it is that the social organisation and simple orderliness of a secondary school can allow.

It is significant that young teachers who, for instance, when they are asked what kind of help they need in their first or second year of teaching in the secondary school, often quote that their problem is mainly that of knowing how to organise a group of pupils whom they wish to move from one end of a school to another in order to take advantage of specialist facilities which the building provides. The simple movement of children itself presents problems not only of discipline but also of the economical use of time. But, otherwise, this points to no very profound moral.

If we assume, however, that a school can cope with the organisational problems of a more diffuse pattern of pupil use of specialist areas, we still have to resolve the problem of deciding the name and purpose of this space and of that. It is of little use talking of studios and of closed circuit television, of carrels and resource learning areas; it is not very helpful to assume that children will instinctively know how to use slide projectors or tape recorders on their own. We know, of course, that children of secondary school age – and even primary school age – are nowadays highly competent in their use of sophisticated electronic machines. Normally, however, these are things which are associated with leisure and not with schooling. The degree to which a child can take a tape recorder seriously in order to advance his learning is different from the way in which he may make use of a tape recorder or cassette player in order to enliven his own leisure hours. Given, however, that the problems of transfer of interest can be overcome, there remains the problem of deciding whether a school is to go over to full pupil-based learning or whether it is enough to allow or encourage teachers to modify their approaches as pupil attitudes – and school opportunities – permit, in a gradual manner.

In making this kind of choice, what is the place of new materials, new explanations of method and new learning resources in themselves? One of the best critiques about the way in which pupil-centred materials for active and individualised learning can be prepared has been written by L. C. Taylor (*Resources for learning*, 1971). One of the morals which he draws is given in an answer to the question of why innovation refuses to stick.

An excess of publicity and persuasion – in contrast to a slow rate of absorption – is something which is bound to lead to frustration and failure. Taylor pleads for what he calls steady dissemination, for detailed books, for word of mouth explanations by practising teachers, and for in-service training on a liberal scale. He also argues that steady local support is essential. If teachers want to try something new because they are under a great deal of pressure from publicists and others, they may achieve, simply, a flurry of interest. Money is voted for a year or two by a local education authority for a particular innovation, for particular equipment and perhaps for one or two brief courses of in-service training; to be open-minded and far-sighted is good – but to continue with the grind of innovation once the initial glamour is over is the challenging part. Teachers find that without the resources which the originators of a particular idea enjoyed on a national scale, they locally cannot persist without the risk of deep personal frustration.

What is often forgotten when the talk about the support of innovation turns to resources is that what is old will often pay its way more effectively than what is new. Because anyone who is interested in the management of change has to believe that what is new has much to be said for it, he is bound to argue with a certain anxiety for novelty for its own sake. Unless he is aware of the levels of energy which are required in terms of finding resource for novelty as well as resource for supporting that which is established and which has proved itself, he is likely to underestimate the whole problem of assistance, support, guidance and morale.

But to return to L. C. Taylor: it is better to persist with old ways than to embark on a muddle of old and new if neither is done properly. Essential alterations seem to be less a matter of large sums of money than of intentions, attitudes and organisations. Innovations can survive in traditional institutions, whether they be schools or colleges of further education. To survive, they need to have experimental pressures applied to them. They cease to survive when pressures are lifted. Again, what works on a small scale becomes difficult, intricate and over-complex when it is extended to a large scale. The feasibility study is easy, the first trial is straightforward; the sustained trial, the working prototype, however, presents problems of survival, stamina and straightforward persistence. These require resources about which we at present know little.

Summary

The management of innovation presents, then, considerable problems for the in-service education of teachers. Differences will be felt as a result of the 1972 White Paper; some of its most significant recommendations are those which deal with the continuous education of teachers. If we are to think of teaching as truly professional, as something in which that which is out of date has no place and in which each of us has a continuous responsibility to young people for the modernity and for the appropriateness of their education, then continuous retraining is an unavoidable necessity.

Many of the items which have been referred to in this chapter fall within the area where curriculum development and educational technology meet. By educational technology here is meant the arrangement of actions and the distribution of resources which will assist reform – against a background of workable ideas about the social and philosophic purposes of improving what children learn.

Training in the handling both of ideas and of resources, training in the making of compromises where sheer facility in either outstrips the other, training in analysing the elements of conflict – each of these represents one facet of the management of resources.

Self-awareness and the observation of others is the start of managing the human part of innovation. What lies beyond the one teacher is, of course, the other human being who can give aid. We have already seen how advisers work in a new context. And alongside the full-time adviser there are others who can be of very direct assistance. The peripatetic teacher of music, the area tutor for drama, the expert handicraft teacher who is employed on a travelling basis as a teacher/tutor or a teacher/adviser in order to take knowledge of new skills or new techniques into schools – all this represents a broad substratum of additional, direct and practical help.

In a primary school the teacher of music who visits for two days a week is misused if his or her time is spent entirely with a small group of pupils. There is a tendency not only for some sort of élitism to build up but also a risk that the skill and expertness which can be brought into school are not used for in-service training. Admittedly there is a convention (and not a very useful one) for a teacher to carry out other work if a peripatetic tutor enters a school. However, the skills of visiting specialists should be used as something which the general teacher (and this is particularly a matter for the primary school) can observe and work with in a more or less unselfconscious manner.

Beyond the adviser and beyond (for want of a better description) 'para-advisory' services, lie those who work locally or regionally with national projects. A wise advisory service and a wise Head can do much to ensure that those who manage national projects – and with whom their own area or school may work – are plugged into the system of local innovation. The outsider who is connected with a larger programme of change or innovation in however particular a field is after all in a better position to see the variety of problems and the variety of needs which have not yet become a matter of awareness for a single school in itself.

Amongst those whose job it is to see a pattern of need and opportunity at some distance from the school are included the men and women who are responsible for school broadcasts. Over the years the supplementary aid which can be given to teachers from radio and television has grown very markedly; more recently television has become a direct method of assisting not only in the classroom but also in the in-service training of teachers.

Between 1970 and 1972 the British Broadcasting Corporation directly extended its further education services to the in-service training of teachers. This had already been successfully done in one or two other professional fields – notably that of medicine. Practical usefulness was the aim and with teachers the attempt was made *not* to launch abstract, discursive or indirect messages. The purpose was to deal with one problem – and as a beginning the area which was treated was that of raising the school leaving age. In order to make as much impact as possible the BBC arranged weekly television sessions of just over half an hour each and a parallel series of sound radio sessions – plus booklets of essays and bibliographies.

The impact of this style of in-service training is difficult to measure; the overall response in the early days was, however, that schools did in a variety of ways find it helpful to have an outside focus for thought and planning about a range of problems which should, admittedly, be fresh – but which had by the early 1970s been talked about for so long that they had become stale.

As a resource in the handling of innovation, the tailor-made TV or sound programme has incomparable benefits. It can take samples and examples from amongst schools whose staffs are facing current problems of preparation and planning. Even so, the BBC (or in fact anybody else who tries very large scale approaches of this kind) faces criticism, doubt and a degree of misunderstanding about what is being aimed at.

A comparable resource, but one which is at present confined to only a few areas, lies in local educational television services. Here the additional resource to which the teacher can turn is that of expert teachers and expert producers of demonstration programmes who aim a message not so much at the teacher but at the pupil. In this, there is obvious side-benefit for the teacher; but ETV is expensive and perhaps will never be able to have the impact in Great Britain which it has had in the United States. The building-up of a network of local television and radio stations is something which is only in its infancy in Great Britain. In the meantime the dangers of ETV are obvious: parochialism, complacency, the overspecialised appeal of a restricted number of messages about innovation to too narrowly drawn a population of teachers – these and other problems about the quality of both level and management of the messages which come through are factors which may place local ETV at some disadvantage in contrast with its national counterpart.

But behind the particularities of new and not yet fully tested ideas, behind inevitable uncertainties about the merit of any one approach to the management of resources, the central importance of retraining is clear. The growing sophistication of our knowledge about those methods which work and those which fail in courses of in-service training enables us gradually to diminish our vagueness and over-optimism about such ideas as professional self-awareness, supportive attitudes, or uncomprehending resistance. If resources are talked about, understood and planned sensibly, other parts of change will fall more easily into place.

The management of training has a great deal to do with the organisation of schools and colleges and with the way in which resources are managed in those institutions. Resources are not entirely matters of textbooks and teaching materials. They are not entirely matters of money and of official support. They are, far more often, matters of attitude and of sympathy.

The way in which teachers can be helped to appreciate (or thoughtfully to reject) what is new depends as much upon their being regarded as those who form a part of a particular organisation as it does upon their being viewed as those who have human feelings, fears, aspirations, prejudices and ambitions.

SUMMARY

It is perhaps a little vague to suggest that the human resource must at all times be the most important one. It certainly sounds more realistic and practical if we commend the study of resources as a process of adding up sums of money, of looking at teacher ratios, examining areas of teaching space. These are important factors in the way in which innovation can be facilitated or retarded. Physical and financial affairs, however, are bound to take second place to the optimism and readiness which a single human being can bring to the task of introducing and sustaining what is new. The management of change after all has far more to do with keeping the thing going than simply with *getting* it going.

The next chapter will look at ways in which a variety of comparatively unstructured reforms have made their impact on schools in England and Wales. The picture will not be a tidy one but it will try to present a portrait of innovation as it now is as well as of how it might turn out.

9 Movements, plans and fashions

The vocabulary and metaphor of change has already been touched upon. Change can be random, development is planned. The language employed in advocating the furtherance of either can depend upon those who are in charge, it can depend upon their sincerity and enthusiasm – and upon their command of other people's interests and loyalty. In managing innovation, those who lead the way can, in some cases, depend on convention and on solid repute. In other cases the innovator has to rely upon idealism and upon spirit rather than on any carefully thought-out intellectual positions which are taken up by those to whom he makes his appeal.

The differences between what is planned and what happens in a less organised fashion can be further sub-divided. Some innovations seem altogether to lack shape, to have many leaders and to change their purposes as time passes. Some developments in curriculum (as well as in school organisation) would be better described as movements. Others, again, are more neatly categorised as plans; yet others are matters of fashion or, more seriously, firm ventures – no more – into territory where there is nothing but uncertainty.

Although there can be nothing hard and fast in the division between the categories of movement, plan and fashion, aspects of management will nevertheless differ according to each category; some examples may reveal what those differences can be.

The movement towards family grouping

The genesis of ideas about family grouping in English primary schools is now a matter of rather vague history. One part of the story lies in the work of Susan Isaacs in the late 1920s and early 1930s. Increasingly loudly it was emphasised at that time that it was important for rein to be given to young children's basic spontaneous interests. A full potential ability (as the phrase put it) existed within each child; how could potential reach fulfilment? One answer was that children in school should be free to find their own level of fulfilment. Restraint should be minimal in the process in which a child moves, as it were, upwards or downwards in finding the right level. And needs were principally expressed in terms of social and personal development rather than as a matter of cognition or of intellectual growth.

Another shaping force lay in the way things were unavoidably organised in small village schools. In large primary schools, the 1862 grip of 'standards' – and hence of rigid streaming – was slow to loosen. In two and three teacher rural schools, however, 'standards' within which children could be grouped homogeneously by age or by ability were impossible to arrange. Younger children had to be educated in the company of older pupils; the dull and the bright, too, had to be taught together.

This definition of dual influences is oversimplified but it gives not too distorted an example of how the effects of more or less rigorous thought, some idealism and simple practical necessity can come together to work towards a common end. For children to be grouped, as it is described, 'vertically' enabled teachers to move away from what now seems the odd rigidity by which one age of child or one ability-level met one teacher and then, at an arbitrary moment of time, moved over to someone else's care.

When it no longer seemed sacrilegious to challenge this rigidity, the idea of family grouping was born. It occurred to teachers that children might sometimes learn better from one another than always from a grown-up, that they might support one another and that they might find both stimulation and comfort in learning at their own pace in the company of older or more knowledgeable children – rather than continually at the pace and behest only of teachers.

What may have been more important than the origin of the movement was, however, the way in which it was progressively handled from decade to decade. Gradually, thoughtful analysis was applied to first ideas; equally gradually, gifted teachers saw the strengths and weaknesses of family grouping, saw the type of learning to which it could best apply – as well as the type to which it had little relevance. Some Heads and assistant teachers emphasised the social value of a design of a school day by which children might learn in a context which more or less truly reflected the atmosphere of a family. Others insisted that cognitive purposes had a primacy over what is social or affective. But whichever way the idea was handled, the movement revealed how improvements could be made.

Family grouping has its bad moments: these tend to occur when schools are exclusive in their adherence to one style of organisation or when those needs of children which can only be properly met by adults are ignored – or when the way in which leadership within a pupil group deteriorates into something which would not be tolerated in the best of families.

Much that is done within vertical grouping is naturally done, as a beginning, experimentally – and then consolidated when teachers gain confidence. This grows as the particular benefit which has been brought to individual children becomes more obvious. But a teacher's confidence also increases as she understands and goes through those preliminary steps of preparation which are necessary if vertical grouping is introduced in place of a more traditional school organisation. That preparation depends on the straightforward planning of such things as the allocation of children and teaching spaces to particular teachers, on deciding how equipment is to be allocated between groups, on the rearrangement of record-keeping, and on settling the school's programme of daily work in such a way that the greatest benefit can be drawn from individual teachers' skills. To these manageable steps of planning two advocates (Ridgway and Lawton) would add the need to inform parents of what is going on, to help children themselves to understand the change, and to provide time for changes to be accepted and consolidated.

In some ways the movement towards family grouping represents a classic method by which teaching and learning can improve in English primary schools. It cancels or by-passes such ill-effects as result from the streaming of children by age or by ability, it goes further than that type of non-streaming which concentrates only on a mixture of children's abilities (without the mixing of age-groups) and it is less exposed to the divisiveness of vertical grouping by ability – where, that is, children of different ages are mingled but where levels of attainment are the main deciding factor in the organisation of pupil-groups.

The movement, too, is gradual. It has about it a quality that is natural. There is nothing forced, nothing excessively theoretical, nothing over-idealistic about the way in which changes are made. Speed is not important and not too much has been claimed in the name of reform at any particular point.

In contrast, however, to the success which family grouping has achieved in the education of the fives to sevens, the projection of this type of organisation into that area of school planning which affects the sevens to ten year olds or, even more complicated, the middle school pupil (8–12 or 9–13 years) presents difficulties. Partly the trouble lies in the fact that junior schooling in England and Wales has in fifty years moved forward less liberally than infant education; second, the emergence of children's differing capacities, speeds of development and future potential is thought to be more marked at the age of nine or ten than it was three years earlier. Hence teachers feel a heavier weight of responsibility for any – as they see it – experimentation which might prejudice a child's chances at the stage of secondary education.

But these sources of difficulty are more deeply rooted in long-established assumption than in the realm of unalterable truth. To say this is not to ignore the importance of certain things having been organised in a particular way for a long period – but longevity on its own provides only repute rather than an ultimate justification for a long-standing activity. However, to advance ideas about vertical grouping in order to meet the needs of children other than those infants with whom the idea originally worked well is not simply an exercise of pitching a novelty in front of resistant Heads or assistant teachers. It is, rather, a piece of work which tests the process of management quite severely.

What is it that is actually beneficial about vertical grouping? Can one essence be distilled from the large and not very clearly defined virtues that have been claimed for the system? Is it clearly known how much of the success of vertical grouping depends on good leadership, how much on certain kinds of training and experience on the part of teachers? What weight should be attached to experience – whether it is the experience of teachers or of parents? These are questions which are bound to be asked when a change is sought which extends the influence of a nebulous movement rather than of a precise strategy. And here, 'nebulous' and 'precise' do not describe meritorious or undesirable qualities: they simply indicate the shape of a practice.

The majority of good practices in English education *are* nebulous. Hence there is difficulty, often, in building out from them. There is also difficulty in transplanting them to other societies. Part of the difficulty which goes with what is nebulous may result from the fact that ideas and practices which are precise can be grasped by simple minds, whereas ideas which carry an essential penumbra of associated ideas and values call for insight and sensitivity before they can be understood and used. These are rarer qualities in the practitioner – and qualities which fit less neatly into theories about management.

The unassuming nature of the achievement of those who depend on gradualist policies is attractive. It has modesty about it and it has a lack of pedantry. But whether one can rely upon the progress of gradual movements of reform as a means of producing a sufficiently widespread or rapid mode of innovation is doubtful. There can be too much shapelessness, too little definition. And although people can do things more or less unconsciously (even if they do them well), they run the risk of acting in a manner which they cannot either rationalise or defend. When they cannot say over-clearly what they do or why they do it, there is the risk that even the minimum degree of rigour in planning and in execution will be missing. Pragmatism is one thing, sustained gradualism is another. When they join, they may produce something that is totally efficient and very acceptable, very human and yet seemingly undemanding. The risks, on the other hand, are those of an over-facile assurance. People can become too cosy about doing what comes naturally.

Family grouping is not a unique example of the type of movement of reform which has brought benefit to English education. It is, however, a clear example of something different from a planned reform, even if only because its history has been so prolonged. The way in which Heads and others change to a style of managing their pupils' learning which depends on family grouping is something which can scarcely be described in a language of models and paradigms.

Despite the unstructured nature of those changes which have been associated with the idea of family grouping, some of the effects are far-reaching. The organisation of a pupil's time in many primary schools, for instance, is nowadays described as forming an 'integrated day'. Other descriptions of this organisation have called it the Free Day. Again, it is something which goes back to Susan Isaacs, the Maltinghouse School, and beyond. In essence it means that within a framework of fixed events in which children have to participate as a group (music, religious education, physical education, the use of TV, drama, dance), the whole day is given over to the pursuit by individual children of activity which is self-chosen.

As a way of organising learning, the integration of activity time depends on the assumption that children enjoy doing congenial things. If they are allowed to follow a chosen line of activity in their own time, they will gradually lose the sense of difference between work and play. Not only will they come to enjoy the traditionally free and enjoyable pursuits of art, craft and other creative work but they will also be cheerful in less obviously palatable activities. The motivation to work and to learn will, together, be heightened.

The way in which the learning of one thing impinges on and overlaps with another is, again, more natural in the small than in the large primary school. Larger schools have a greater separation between teachers and classes; time in the past has had to be more strictly compartmentalised in order to make the organisation workable. But habits change and by now the benefits of a more free timetable can be appreciated by teachers in large as well as in small schools. However, the size and juxtaposition of classrooms together with traditional ways or organising staff sometimes make it difficult to prevent children's time from being too neatly sliced up into separated lessons, occasionally with different teachers and with too few chances for an interest to be pursued to a conclusion which satisfies the child rather than the timetable. Because in a system of family grouping children come together and stay together – diverse in their interests, speed of work and capacities – the need to have a flexible timetable is virtually unavoidable. And family grouping, particularly with infants but also (though less easily) with children of junior age, makes it more practicable for larger schools to organise an 'integrated day'.

The interdependence of these two slow-acting reforms in English primary education need not be laboured. Each helps the other; both are examples of change where the initiation could not in a very strict sense be 'managed'. Schools see a chance to do something and lessons are learned from others who have attempted things earlier; success depends on the Head of a school gauging the readiness of his staff, on his formulating clear ideas about accommodation, capitation allowances, timetable and the degree to which – by a combination of energy, insight and resources – an idea can be made to work.

The effects of a movement which is handled in this way can mingle with a planned innovation. Such a movement, for instance, as the desire to drop selection and to change over to unstreamed teaching – this can be quoted as something which is by now part of an accepted movement and which also has behind it a certain amount of planning and idealistic zeal.

Those who advocate that certain benefits of this type should apply more widely to the education of our children often, however, have in addition to a pedagogic purpose an aim which is more clearly social. Comparably, again, one can look at team teaching and at the desire not only that teachers should work as teams but also that differences between disciplines and subjects should gradually become rather less visible than in the past. These latter examples, however, fall into the category not so much of a movement as of deliberately planned reform.

Planned reform: team teaching

Unlike the way in which innovation is managed when it has its origins in one central national project, changes which come about in the way in which non-streaming has been introduced into English schools or the manner in which interdisciplinary work has found favour – each of these represents a mixture of the movement of ideas, the growth of favour for certain styles of thinking, a degree of hard planning, a certain amount of social as opposed to purely pedagogic learning and a gradually changing readiness for new styles of organisation in particular classes on the part of particular teachers.

The management of innovation in this context has to cover such a variety of styles of work and has to account for so many differing purposes which the advocates of change wish to serve, that it is difficult to speak very clearly about how anyone should make the most of what is strong or avoid what is weak.

In team teaching both strength and weakness is apparent. It became comparatively well-known in Britain in the early-to-mid-1960s. At that time the principal lessons to be learned came from the United States of America. One or two detailed and critical accounts of the way in which team teaching was managed in the United States not only warned of the perils of expecting too much but also despite pessimism, gave the feeling that there was much to be gained from looking upon a number of teachers as people who might be capable of working as a team – and in something more than spirit.

The Plowden Report did not take team teaching very seriously insofar as it might benefit primary schools. It dismissed it fairly lightly by expressing the assumption that teachers of younger children were already accustomed to working together. But Plowden also commended English schools for making it possible for teachers to co-operate without sacrificing the framework of firmly organised classes and classrooms. A critic of Plowden on this point (such as John Freeman) would say that the reference to firm frameworks of class teaching as a background to the team approach reveals confusion or possible misunderstanding of the method.

It is because the team approach appears to have a clear definition (which we can defend, attack, or argue about) that it is best treated as a development which lacks the more nebulous elements of ideas which have grown, like family grouping, more or less organically.

It can be claimed that from Froebel onwards there has been a progression of ideas about team teaching. Those who have attempted to loosen up school organisation by emphasising that teachers need not insist on continuing to be individually autonomous and self-contained have always come near to some kind of central message about team strategies. Those who, comparably, have argued in favour of a core curriculum and for a better integration between subjects have also appealed to the idea of teachers planning and working together, making their efforts complementary to each other.

At its broadest, the idea that teachers can add to the flexibility of their school's organisation – if they are only given the chance to co-operate and plan in a co-ordinated manner – sounds very much like the argument that was, earlier, used about family grouping and about the timetabling of the so-called integrated day. It may be because there are several points at which ideas cross each other's boundaries that the Plowden Report said what it did. Anyone who wishes to defend team teaching as something relatively new and different as well as more controlled and defined, has to look for one definitive element as a point of origin.

Freeman (*Team teaching in Britain*) looks to Lloyd Trump in 1959. At that date he argued for a better use of teachers' own knowledge and abilities; he argued too for the child to have an enlarged opportunity of learning. In order that schools might do something about both these points it would, argued Trump, be necessary to think hard about dividing children's activities in school between those which were best arranged for large groups, those which demanded small groups and those other activities which were inevitably a matter for individual pupils. He also urged that there should be a clearer sense amongst teachers about what went on in the actual process of teaching. The teacher inspires pupils and gives them information. The way in which teachers do this needed, thought Trump, to be re-examined.

Secondly, he felt that it was necessary to look again at what children do when the teacher withdraws. Ideally withdrawal should lead to independent study. If it happens at all, independent study itself works in a variety of ways – quite separately carried on by individual children, or conducted in pupils' own (unsupervised) groups, or again separately (pupil by pupil) but under a light supervision, or finally in a group – but again with light supervision.

In one sense, then, a few basic messages about team teaching seemed originally to be that it would (in England, at least) be of more concern to secondary than to primary schools, that it necessitated a rearrangement (by the school as a whole) of time allocations, group sizes and accommodation, and it necessitated a reconsideration by individual teachers of the ways in which children learn. The starting point in some ways is not too far from present-day statements about individualised learning. Nor was team teaching in the early days easy to disentangle from questions about the management of resources. The management of learning overall, in fact, played a large part in the thinking of Trump and others as the label of team teaching came to take on its apparently specific meaning.

That one can talk about the definition as being only 'apparently specific' reveals a confusion. Those who enthuse about team teaching as though it were a single idea, method or approach tend to talk about it as though there truly was, within a limited and identifiable period of time, a single beginning. Because of the assumption that it is a single entity, advocates behave as they would if what was being discussed was, say, a national reform project, with a single field and a single purpose. If it were such a reform, the manner of describing it would quite appropriately be that of planned innovation. But the process of spreading out those arguments which lead teachers to accept the benefits of team teaching are unlike the process of diffusing information about a single project. And in its application at school level, team teaching does require very detailed planning.

So far, these same comments could be made about family grouping – which has been categorised as a movement rather than as a plan. Despite the fact that both ideas are in some ways concerned with very comparable purposes, those which lie behind team teaching call for a sense of once-for-all commitment (even if the whole system is later dropped) while, in contrast, family grouping and the integrated day can make a gradual impact. This may be possible because there is a certainty about some benefits which schools can afford to take in their stride.

Team teaching may, by contrast, not be totally good or capable of being efficiently handled. A teacher's nerve may therefore need to be made more resolute before the attempt. If an activity needs nerve, it needs decisiveness.

When schools decide to take the step towards team teaching they can base their decisions either on, say, three Trump-like arguments (about groups and individuals, teacher-direction and independent learning, the better use of resources) or on arguments in favour of interdisciplinary study. The latter alternative recurs, reports Freeman, in secondary schools' accounts of why – and to some extent how – they have introduced team teaching. As an example the work of Mrs Charity James on interdisciplinary enquiry (IDE) at Goldsmith's College in London from the mid-1960s has clearly done much both to inspire teachers with the wish to involve pupils more directly in their learning and to give them a confident knowledge of techniques which can give help.

The number of accounts which have been written about the introduction of team teaching into particular schools now adds up to a respectable corpus. A point-by-point analysis of reports would here only repeat what has been done elsewhere. What is worth noting, however, is the moral which each description carries for the management of introducing a change of method. One person takes an initiative; if that person is not himself the Head, the Head has to bless the initiative – and usually by taking part in subsequent activity rather than by simply nodding wisely. When the change is justified, it is argued about not as mere method but as an activity which is central to the content and style of children's learning – affecting their motivation, understanding, self-reliance, maturation and capacity to internalise new experiences. This inevitably adds to the prestige of the change and makes it more difficult for those teachers who are less interested to be openly cynical. Thirdly, the introduction has to be accompanied by rearrangement of timetables and spaces; children have to be clearly prepared and the novelty has not only to be explained to parents but also to win their acquiescence.

Planned reform: integrated studies

Much of what was first said in favour of team teaching came at a time when those who were teaching in secondary schools were ready to look seriously at resources. In the mid-1960s, after all, we were facing what then seemed a customary crisis of teaching power. Certain secondary subjects were apparently destined to remain in the category of 'shortage subjects'. If there were always to be too few teachers of modern languages or religious education, then the skills of those who were already in employment should be better used by allowing them to affect the learning of a larger number of pupils than simply by working through the timetable of thirty pupils at a time in a box of limited size. Thus, team teaching came when we were concerned about the human resources of education and at a time, too, when we were ready to break down a few of the barriers between subjects.

To teach as a team or to lower the division between subjects calls for a certain type of democracy which is not always found in English schools. Differences must be sunk in order to achieve some common purpose.

Not all schools need to see that the sinking of differences between teachers is a good thing. After all, many of the great traditions of English education have sprung from the efforts of those who have idiosyncrasies and special skills, from those who are unique and who are not afraid to let their uniqueness affect their way of doing things. Nevertheless team teaching was something which had benefits which could be planned for.

In some ways the coincidence is a confusing one between the fashion for team teaching and the separately encouraged development of integrated, interrelated or interdisciplinary study. In the simplest sense team teaching is a matter of organisation: but unless it is clear which are the strengths which teachers shall give to a team – and why – there is little to be gained by complicated timetabling and a possibly confusing variation in the size of pupil-groups.

Where did a practical interest in team teaching originate? In 1963 the Newsom Report confirmed the long-suspected lack of interest which pupils in the later years of compulsory secondary education hold for subjects which they and their parents do not regard as vocationally useful. It can be easily recognised why religious education, music, civics and history were included amongst the subjects which engendered boredom. Yet there are elements in these subjects which should form a proper part of an adolescent's education. Could these most essential – or useful – elements be extracted, brought together and taught within one framework?

The question is in itself complicated. Employers expect schools to make pupils competent in English and in some form of mathematics. Is education to achieve other and less clearly useful ends? If so, do those other subjects (RE, history, music, etc.) contribute to those ends?

Examples of attempts to define ends, aims and purposes which do not relate to practice are commonplace. If we say straightforwardly that schooling should teach the pupil how to learn – and that learning should not be confined to choices made by teachers, everyone will understand. The school must then find the best answer, in single subjects or through integration, through the work of separate teachers or through team teaching. Whichever answer is found and whichever the medium through which curriculum is intended to work, teachers have to be clear how learning in one sphere relates to another.

One way by which we learn more (and by which we learn to learn) is by developing our capacity to apply to a new situation, problem, or activity a particular insight or piece of knowledge which we have acquired in another field. The process of applying an acquired skill to a new field is much argued about; the usual language is that of the transfer of learning. Arguments go deep (and long) into the extent to which learning can indeed be transferred between differing fields of activity; however, despite long argument, most education depends for its justification on the idea that there *is* a transfer value.

Those who want to move away from traditional puzzles about transfer usually examine the basic structures of school subjects and try to pick out a significant type of knowledge which *generates* fresh knowledge. In the effort to determine which parts of knowledge should in this way take priority, the working processes of, for instance, historians and biologists matter more than what is simply *said* about history and biology in textbooks: information about subject matter which is merely selected for the pupil varies in significance. If, however, the process of a historian's thinking can be genuinely shared with and taken over by the child, this may enable us to penetrate further into problems about the use of knowledge. In particular we may be able to find out something about the cross-application which a child makes between what he newly learns and what he already understands.

The process by which something is thought out or by which fresh knowledge is acquired differs in an obvious way from the idea that the content of a child's learning is simply static. Some indeed will argue (and very persuasively) that if a child can learn something about the process of acquiring knowledge, of solving problems, of making choices, and of cross-applying what is learned – this in itself should be part of the content of education.

Arguments in support of these lines of thought and practice are refined and careful. They make the usual divisions between content and method appear crude and limited in their usefulness. But in particular the merits of the argument of those who urge us to think of 'process as content' rest heavily on the need to marry theory (about learning processes and about learning structures) with the observed practices of those who teach. What is new must gain acceptance by the teaching profession and by those who, in laymen's manner, have responsibility for public education. Here, theory on its own is not enough.

It is, of course, the theory about cross-applications and about the interdisciplinary nature of learning which is the weakest point. Those who operate systems of shared teaching in secondary schools in support of the interdisciplinary idea face themselves, as we have already seen, with organisational problems. But they also have philosophic problems – if, that is, they feel responsibility for proving some authenticity for their plans. If, for instance, a teacher wishes to define what he wants to do with history in an interdisciplinary plan of teaching, he first needs some kind of answer to the more difficult question of what history itself does; why does it exist as a subject? What can it achieve as a discipline of thought?

If the teacher of history proposes to contribute to an interdisciplinary curriculum, he has to satisfy those with whom he shares his plans. He will have to answer questions about the way in which history (in a manner not shared with other disciplines) can help people to verify data, to work towards conclusions of thought, and to estimate the importance (and truth, too) of evidence.

Although the teacher needs more or less 'pure' philosophic answers to these questions he will only find them pedagogically usable if he bases his work on observing how pupils take things in, how they manipulate them and how they apply them.

These three parts of the process do not all seem to be of equal importance to those who practise interdisciplinary teaching in the primary school. The first two aspects (intake and manipulation) are matters to which a great deal of attention is admittedly paid in the teaching of language and of early mathematics. How children listen and understand, how they identify and categorise – these are central to both areas of activity. In the same way the manipulative side receives due attention: teachers in primary schools spend much time and attention in helping their pupils to verify, compare and interpret what they learn.

The aspect of work which receives less attention is that of application: how do children make decisions, construct new ideas or find solutions to problems which have both finality and satisfaction?

If the teacher of young children baulks at this, it is understandable. Maturity and a well-developed range of learned skills are necessary for much of the work. But students in secondary education should possess both maturity and skills: hence there should be little difficulty in assuming that teachers can look at all three aspects of any subject – whether separately or in an interdisciplinary framework. There should be equally little difficulty in assuming that teachers will marry theory with practical observation when they set out to prove the authenticity of what they do.

But, of course, issues are never clear-cut. There will be differentiation in achievement between pupils and between subjects. Some of the difference will depend on industriousness. Or it will matter whether the child has what the subject needs – a good memory, or natural skill or even stamina. Again, if pupils prefer the rewards of status to those of pleasure, the management of their teaching ought to differ.

If differences between pupils' responses to subjects matter when those subjects are taught separately, they will make things even more complicated if an attempt is made at some style of integration of study. To manage well any development in this aspect of curricular work – as in others – will depend on justifications about practice, on philosophic argument, on teachers' thoroughness in observation and planning and on what can still be described as the fine art of teaching. Can the teacher see to which of his qualities individual pupils will respond at any one time? Can he bring these qualities into play in a manner which elicits the best response from the largest number of pupils? And can a group of teachers, working through several subjects, exercise the art with the same sensitivity as an individual teacher? Can the necessary skills be shared? If so, can sharing be achieved in any way other than intuitively? Can good management give help or act as a substitute? And if so, will this be management which depends on plans and procedures, a management scheme in fact which can apply in more than a limited number of circumstances? Or will the success of integrated study be so dependent upon the art of teaching that management in any significant sense has no place?

The subtle interplay between the things that matter in integrated studies make it ironic that the dilemma has at any stage to be crudely posed as management versus personal skill. But even if no way can be found of reducing the subtleties, this type of curriculum development has to be recognised as being virtually indefinable. The aim is an improvement in education – in terms of process, subject matter and method. It is even doubtful whether we could confine it within the terms of curriculum alone.

We ought to be able to talk in a reasonable and credible way about the management, here, of integrated studies. However, even if we cannot, it has to be accepted that the study of society or of what humanity owes to science or, say, of how maths, the sciences and history interconnect – that these are proper studies. We may be in a primitive state of achieving interconnections between subjects which are well-defended as separate studies – and the defenders of tradition may be justified in repelling ill-thought-out or jargon-loaded plans for interdisciplinary work. But we cannot risk losing potential benefit, even if at present incoherent or poorly judged arguments are used in order to explain them. The potential benefit had been clearly indicated in 1963 when the Newsom Report advocated that the teaching of conventional subjects in secondary schools should be re-examined. We had been reminded that not all children found school to be very relevant to their sense of adult need. Schools were places where there might be some boredom. Schools, too, were institutions where children could not see the point of having watertight divisions between history or civics, or modern languages, or RE.

So far, then, the way in which integrated work in secondary schools has been handled has sometimes lived up to the promise of those who were its earliest advocates. But what has come to the forefront is not so much a concern for the lowering of boundaries as for the evolution of fresh ways in which subject areas might be approached. In one sense, part of this has been referred to in earlier comments about the Humanities Curriculum Project. Ideas can be formalised, arrangements can be made with teaching staffs and in the time allocations of secondary schools. Even accommodation can be handled in such a way that support can be given to an idea which might distinctly pay off in terms of eliciting greater interest (and in reviving the enthusiasm) of teachers. To plan the use of staff, time and space is important too in enforcing a review of the purposes and methods of teaching subjects which, in their separated condition, were perhaps making too little impact.

However, there are at the same time obvious weaknesses in some interdisciplinary work; some of these originate in mismanagement. If too much reliance is placed on initiatives which particular teachers can take, if too much is left to informal arrangement between heads of departments or between individual assistant teachers, if not enough attention is paid to time, space, facilities and to the careful routine planning of interdisciplinary courses, failure will be inevitable.

In one sense the single lesson of which management here has to take note is that interdisciplinary work is extremely demanding on human resource; it is unlikely to succeed, at least in the first instance, if it is attempted over too long a period. The process of planning must allow teachers to see the end to which they are working. Efforts should not be spread over too many terms nor should purposes be nebulous. Because these simple aspects of short term planning have been lost sight of, many efforts at interdisciplinary work have (although appearing grandiose) so far remained ineffective. And, again, if teachers are asked to strive towards a goal which always seems beyond reach, they lose faith in their capacity.

Planned reform: non-streaming

The success of management in making things appear tangible, attainable and practicable applies to non-streaming. The movement here is again a mixture of idealism, social purpose and pedagogic benefit. Ideas about this style of organisation in secondary schools again took their roots from North American rather than in British practice. Again we have had difficulties about cross-cultural transfer – despite the success of non-streaming (like integrated learning and vertical grouping) over many years in a large number of rural British primary schools.

In spite of difficulties, however, those Heads who wish to unstream first, second or third years of secondary schools usually have good purposes. They are able to explain what they wish to do not only to the satisfaction of their assistant staff but also to parents who are unaccustomed to thinking that heterogeneous levels of ability can be handled within unified teaching groups. Despite goodwill, however, many plans for altering traditional structures of streaming have come to grief because too much has been asked of teaching staff in too short a time.

The purpose behind an innovation which is meant to reduce social barriers and which is meant to prove the Pygmalion effect of higher expectations on children whose attainment has previously been thought to be potentially low – this combination of hope and aspiration carries inherent risks. While very few people would be surprised if children of mixed abilities were unable to work together in handicrafts or in physical education or in expressive subjects such as music and art, equally few people would be surprised if mixed ability grouping were something which could with ease and practicality be applied to languages, or mathematics or certain kinds of science.

It is, of course, in this latter trinity of subjects that most Heads who attempt to alter the streaming of their first three years in a secondary school come to grief; egalitarianism and differences of ability clash. Non-streaming carries risks of slow progress for students who have a special potential in certain fields. By the same token, the mixing of abilities creates frustration and a sharper sense of failure for those who are less able.

There is the added stress, of course, that cognitive achievement is, whatever else may be claimed, held to be more significant than attainment in non-cognitive areas of the curriculum. Hence to introduce heterogeneous groups of ability in the teaching of essentially cognitive subjects (if there are truly any such), heightens the sense of difference. And, as so often when an aim cannot be perfectly achieved, any re-examination of effectiveness or alteration of strategy focuses not on the modification of methods but on the redefinition of aims. Because of this the reaction to any change of circumstances is not to drop the language of non-streaming but to modify it.

We then come most naturally to the idea of 'setting'. Children are much of a muchness for a large part of the curriculum (and can be unstreamed, safely) but have to be brought together in more uniform groups of ability for subjects which are intellectually demanding.

One of the curiosities of innovation in this style of organising children's learning is that nobody seems too upset about self-contradictions in claiming at one moment to treat children as though they could learn in a homogeneous fashion when they are, in fact, soon separated into disparate groups according to the difficulty of individual subjects.

Typically, then, a secondary school which claims to have unstreamed any of its years will have common learning groups for non-cognitive subjects and selected, hierarchical, differentially organised groups for more demanding parts of the curriculum. And when 'setting' creates difficulties, we defend the democratic nature of learning by using another idea, that of 'banding'. Again what is aimed at is some kind of organisational breadth. Children are not to be divided, they are to be grouped in a way which diminishes the importance of recognising the capacity which some people have of learning more quickly or more effectively than others.

In recent years in Britain the expression of cynicism about the way in which changes of ability grouping are organised in many of our secondary schools has been confined largely to the so-called Black Papers. However, even apart from their kind of attack, there are research studies in plenty which seem to show that children know what their levels of ability are; they are seldom surprised at the labels which are attached by teachers within particular subject areas.

Non-streaming is not simply a 'movement'. It has about it elements of plan and of a purpose which extend beyond pedagogy to the realm of social ideal. The management of change here is something which must avoid risks of being patronising, artificial or too self-conscious. The de-streaming of a school at the secondary school age is something which can only really work if labels and categorisations have been avoided at some much earlier period. If, however, children are accustomed – as they seem to be in so many primary schools – to knowing whether they are potential successes or failures at the age of eight or nine, then it seems unrealistic to hope that certain new styles of organisation can cancel out their sense of frustration at a later stage. Some almost superhuman quality of planning is required in order to make the most of this kind of innovation.

Broader participation in reform

Three examples which have so far been briefly dealt with draw their attractiveness from claims about an ideal of democracy and the reduction of social divisions.

In common with the movement towards reducing the apparent differences between people, the idea that as many as possible should take part in the planning and execution of public activities now has considerable support. Jargon has built up quickly in the language of participation. The language is fashionable, and fashion can of course produce change. Is it, however, a type of change which can be managed – or is it something which must simply take its own shape in its own time?

With the 1974 changes in the organisation of local government in England and Wales the principal benefits for education are that more people will know more about what is being done within the system. Those in charge, too, are intended to be more accountable for their activities – and we should have a better sense of connection between the purposes of community activity at large and the process of educating people in the mass.

Education is one of the few local government services in England and Wales which is scrutinised frequently. As a result of many commissions, reports, and other papers from Central Advisory Councils it is something which is almost continuously being modernised. Modernisation always poses alternatives. Is education to be brought up to date in terms of teaching method, curriculum and general quality? Or is it to be provided for more people? Although it is often assumed that both types of improvement cannot be afforded at the same time, efforts continue to be made simultaneously.

In England and Wales, the history of improving people's access to education and of allowing more students to learn for longer periods should have meant that there is by now a wider understanding about the nature of education than existed when it was, for instance, something which only a minority of people could enjoy beyond the age of fourteen. But stereotypes take a long time to change; although education is more widely sought after year by year, there is little evidence that it is looked at very differently by succeeding generations of parents, students, or teachers.

If education as a local authority service is to become better understood, there are two needs which have to be met. From one point of view, more families should be helped to understand the possible benefits of an extended education – and how to secure these benefits for their children. From another, more people should be helped to understand why education has to be constantly improved, how this is attempted and what is its likely cost.

The Plowden Report in 1967 said a great deal about the way in which parents might be more closely involved in what went on in schools. It was felt that if a parent took more interest in how his child was being taught, some degree of support for learning at home would accelerate the child's learning at school. This led to the advocacy of the greater involvement of parents in both the curricular and social aspects of school life.

This is what, in small-scale terms of school improvement, has to be set against the larger background of the Royal Commission report on local government reform. The bigger perspective of what matters is seen not so much in particularities of curriculum or of teaching method but in a total involvement of communities in the quality of planning and in the conduct of public activities. Education is simply one such activity – expensive, difficult to understand or to explain – and the difficulty makes it harder to promote the idea of a wider public participation in education's advancement.

The broad idea that participation should indeed be public had admittedly been carefully sketched out in the report of a national committee (Skeffington), which in the late 1960s had examined the methods by which the work of planning authorities could be a matter of civic sharing. It has been hoped, amongst other things, that more attention would be paid to the way in which young people might be trained to recognise the levers of power in

BROADER PARTICIPATION IN REFORM

their own communities and that they might be trained, too, to pull those levers at the time when the quality of community life might otherwise suffer.

The response from within the education service to this definition of participation has so far been fairly sketchy. One of the few signs of activity or interest has come from those who have concern for the government of schools. This, alongside the growth of better informal connections between parents and schools after the Plowden Report, represents an interest in a more constitutional relationship between school and community, a participation by voting, by committee procedure and by other appurtenances of formal activity.

The government of schools in England and Wales is a matter of history which has at times been interesting, sometimes acrimonious and at other times merely time-consuming. Until 1902 the government of schools was something in which central government took an interest. Governing bodies and managing bodies were those to whom grant was payable and who were in one way or another responsible for the quality and efficiency of education which was provided at the state's expense. In 1902, however, after the introduction of local education authorities into the educational scene, the power of governors and managers diminished. Local education authorities took over many of the rights which affected the quality of education in terms of, for instance, curriculum and the appointment of teaching staff.

From time to time since 1902 attempts have been made to enlarge and restore some of the pristine authority of governors. These efforts have not been successful. The 1944 Education Act diminished, still further, what was left. Governors and managers by now have very little say, financial or otherwise, in anything which affects the school. They have (apart from some teaching appointments in Aided schools) little to say about the way in which staff are appointed. They nevertheless do retain a formal role in the appointment of staff – and particularly in the appointment of Heads of schools. Even then, however, they markedly play a lesser role than local education authorities.

In the way that governors and managers have been relegated to a position of less influence, few people find very much to object to. However, the fact that their historical and social position was once something firmly established in the British educational scene accounts for the manner in which some people would like to see action taken to restore the effectiveness of very local bodies of influence in the school system.

There are some who hope that local government reorganisation will restore to governors their one-time distinct advisory power, when national systems of communication and national ideas about democracy were very different from those of the present day.

Until recently, parents of children in attendance at a school were not necessarily represented on governing and managing bodies. This has been put right to a large extent by the activities of local education authorities who have followed the advice of the Plowden Report. The good effects have been felt in both secondary and primary schools. And the movement has now extended beyond the representation of parents to the idea that pupils themselves should have a voice in school government.

Pupil power, as the jargon describes this movement, is something which may one day prove to be a valuable innovation in the way in which education is conducted. It might, ideally, mean that education could become child-centred – to the extent that children actually had a say in what they should be taught. It might even be taken to the point that children had a say in what they consented to *learn*. However, the cultural tradition of education in England and Wales seems to go against the forecast about the speed with which the voice of the pupil or the student can be heard; education is basically adult-centred and adult-directed – because it is expected to be like that.

Admittedly in one or two colleges of art and increasingly in polytechnics and universities, the voice of students in matters which relate to curricular and social organisation has been more clearly heard. The voice was usually first audible in an atmosphere of acrimony and indecisiveness on the part of those who by tradition governed these institutions. It was against the background of disconcertedness, surprise and resentment that arguments about student power were brought into play. But things have gradually changed and the student voice in college government is now more readily accepted.

If college students successfully win the right to participate in the government of their college, should the sixth formers of a comprehensive school be represented on the governing body? If sixth formers are admitted, should fifth formers be there? If fifth formers are represented, how low down the age range should representation proceed?

In the attempts which are made to answer such questions, one set of arguments is concerned with the maturity and the commonsense of pupils and students who might find themselves in a position of joining with their elders on a governing body. But these issues are less relevant and important than the need to ensure that everyone who is in the debate should be clear as to the purposes of securing a student voice in government. If the voice is something which is sought as a matter of idealism or of an enthusiastic movement which lacks power of persistence, then it hardly seems to be worth making too much fuss. If, however, the voice of the student (as consumer) is to be heard in any significant sense, then a stronger argument arises for claiming that proper account should be taken.

The final outcome of the movement for greater pupil power in schools is as yet unclear. There are, however, signs that the movement is being misunderstood and mismanaged. Action groups which spring up have vivacity and dynamism. This may be misleading; it may be something which burns itself out. There are models from the other side of the Atlantic from which those who foster the student argument may derive encouragement. Mismanagement, however, seems to lie on the side of the adults, and of those who are in authority over schools and colleges. And no one seems to be too certain about the nature of what is being witnessed. It may be a natural movement towards democratic participation. On the other hand it may be a force for which proper planning should be brought into play in order to secure a desirable and important improvement in the government of education. To the cynic, however, it may seem that we are merely watching an interplay of fashions. But how accurately can we identify fashion?

One sign of fad rather than of an established movement lies in the language; it tends to be nebulous, political and idealistic. Secondly, the metaphor of such language is based, as some would describe it, on social rather than on 'architectonic' spheres of human activity – on what passes rather than on what has permanence. Thirdly, the language used by advocates of fashion is governed by emotion rather than by reason. This is not necessarily a sign of shallowness. What is fashionable is by definition – and at its own time – new. Because it is new the description of it has to be couched in language to which we may not be accustomed. New words draw fresh attention to ideas, they make news and, in turn, headlines. Not surprisingly, the popular media make much of movements such as those of student power or, as another instance, of de-schooling.

Ideas which seem at any one moment impermanent can still present significant problems for the management of educational change. The growth of interest in new forms of participation, whether by parents or students, cannot be left entirely to the media, to individual initiatives, or to a process of informal growth.

Admittedly the effect on education of activities which are informal, separated from each other and unsupported by organised pupil interest can, in the manner of the progressive schools of the 1920s and 1930s, be sharp and salutary. But they cannot have a permanent effect unless they are institutionalised. Hence the usefulness of parents and students who share in making policy in education can only be significantly felt if their participation becomes possible on a wide scale. It is better, then, that parents should by *regulation* be required to be represented amongst the governors and managers of schools; sixth formers in the same way as college students must also be given a place which is *reserved* for them by official decree. But to be able to participate as a matter of right places a duty on the participant to be well-informed, constructive and responsible. It is not enough to be merely militant.

The fashion of participation does not appear capable of being left on the periphery of the organisation and politics of education. It represents some alertness about what happens (and about what *might* happen) within the system. It also represents something new and about which more has, in terms of management, still to be learned.

Until they learn their task and take their new responsibility so seriously that they can challenge experts and professionals on their own ground, students and parents can make no significant alteration in the pattern of power and influence in education. We can say this in England with some assurance not because the militancy, persuasiveness, or sincerity of those who act on behalf of parents and students is in question. It is because those whom parents and students try to influence, namely governors and managers, have (in a seventy year tradition) lost their importance. It is doubtful whether any one now either can or needs to revitalise this part of the machine; desuetude has set in. And, even if governors and managers had not already lost their power, for anyone to try to achieve change through broader public participation in that quarter would in any event be wrong. It is not a point at which radical change can be made.

At a time when local government in England and Wales is going through some remarkable reforms it would be reasonable to think that one of the aims of those reforms would apply to education as clearly as it should to the work of social service departments, planning departments and others who in a mixture of democracy and bureaucracy make public decisions which affect our daily lives. The principal purpose of local government reorganisation is to provide, on an up to date scale, access for the public to the business of making decisions. At the same time those who make and act on those decisions ought to become more visibly accountable for what they do.

In these reforms the broader pattern of managing both the static and the developing aspects of education will remain as it has been since 1944; local education authorities which have the same legal and geographical boundaries as the smaller number of new, large 'first tier' authorities will administer a locally determined but (largely) government-financed system. Certain more local sub-divisions of authority, such as Divisional Executives, will disappear. Unless authorities choose to set up some local advisory structure, where the public can get at the machine in order to find things out as well as to show where matters are going wrong, the new system runs the risk of becoming more impersonal than before – and certainly in rural areas.

To provide a fully local contact between parents or other members of the public with the local education authority, it should be possible to strengthen ideas about the *community* responsibility which rests with governors and managers. If they could become a proper point of focus for local interests, where policy could be interpreted to parents and parental wishes interpreted to the local authority, they could achieve a worthwhile but long-absent rapport between small localities and central authorities.

De-schooling

In order to become more radical in questioning whether any improved degree of public contact and participation might change education's quality, we need to turn to the de-schoolers. In many ways, the questions which they pose make matters of management and development appear trivial. Their central concern is with what has been called the modernisation of poverty. Men think rich, live poor – and their impoverishment has many of its roots in compulsory schooling. Schooling is claimed to have an anti-educational effect. It specialises in marking out failures and it constantly shows how costly, difficult (and almost impossible) the task of education really is.

Within the school, it is argued, curriculum is a matter of ritual which was originally intended to separate a child's personal life-chances from his potential life-chances; his opportunities could be improved, his chances equalised. But, the de-schoolers claim, instead of equalising chances schools now simply monopolise their distribution.

The argument goes further: education is desirable but schools cannot provide it. This, the radicals would say, is partly because schools link together experiences of which some seem particularly irrelevant to pupils; partly the reason lies, too, in the way in which skill instruction is not provided – either to the degree or in the activities which pupils want.

De-schoolers do not believe that education should only be a matter of instruction in skills; the place for informal, incidental learning should be very secure with any system of education – but schools are inefficient at providing that type of learning.

Education as something complex, lifelong, and unplanned is something which makes the process of schooling in itself seem artificial. Spontaneity vanishes; and when we learn to live – without much help from a school – this means, the advocates of de-schooling would say, that we learn to speak, to think, to love, to feel, to play, to curse, and to work *outside* school. So what are schools for?

The arguments are not simply nihilistic; but de-schoolers do not believe that schools as compulsory institutions leave children free enough. Schools condition children in readiness for other influences to have an effect – the less benign influences, perhaps, of consumer society. And thus, instead of saying that our task in schools is to prepare children for society in early adulthood, the de-schoolers advocate that by doing away with school we might change society more quickly. We might, they suggest, even get away from the artificial status of 'childhood'. You might be an infant until you could show some usefulness. After that, you could be treated as having grown up.

The criticisms which the de-schoolers make are easy to parody. Nevertheless they are serious indicators of many ailments. For instance, it is crude to typify the curriculum as a matter of commodity and merchandise. This style of description goes too far in assuming that all curriculum reform is a matter of newly packaged materials. But whether they are right or not in criticising curriculum materials, the de-schoolers may ironically be right when they claim that those in education can always justify more costly curriculum work – but only with the effect, as is claimed, that learning difficulties rise proportionately with the cost of curriculum.

Philosophically the de-schooling movement has much to be said for it. It returns to a question which was posed, for instance, by William Taylor some years ago when he said that children attended schools as though they were inmates of a prison – but with a difference that those who attend school, even under a law of compulsion, do so voluntarily. There is no knowing, as Taylor says, at what point all those who attend a school may choose to walk out. They attend, after all, by some contract or convention. There are very few sanctions which can be brought to bear to prevent the mass renunciation of schooling by the majority of children – but the de-schoolers would add that children have less protection from the force of compulsion than the inmates of jails and mental hospitals.

There are in Britain as yet few of the tensions which might lead us to expect gross dissatisfaction with a system of schooling to which people have after all become accustomed over a matter of a hundred years – or more realistically in terms of *mass* education over something like forty years. But there is no benefit in being complacent in the face of threats which originate in other countries or for other reasons. The time could quickly come when the authority of schooling is seriously challenged in England and in Wales. When that happens, it will matter how well those who manage the system will be able to accommodate what now seem to be radical demands and radical threats. If the management of a system cannot accommodate radical change, it will break.

If we reach the stage of thinking seriously about the curricular implications of disestablishing the school or of de-schooling society, it would be worthwhile to see what the alternatives are. It is not to leave society without a means of educating people: it is, however, to remove the idea that education essentially is confined to our younger years, that it is universally compellable and that within it there is an obligatory curriculum.

To learn is a necessary activity for living: hence one, probably the major, proponent of de-schooling (Ivan Illich) recommends a mode of learning which is not entirely either novel or surprising – that of self-motivated learning. The teacher should not be the single funnel through which education is passed to the child.

In arguments which are in some ways comparable to those of L. C. Taylor, the way in which self-motivated learning should be assisted centres on four methods, which make up an 'educational web'. The strands of the web would be a reference service for 'educational objects' (books, museum exhibits, laboratory specimens, artefacts of industry and commerce), a system of 'skill exchange' by which people with special skills which they are prepared to allow others to use would be made known, and a comparable system of 'peer-matching' by which a network of communication might be established in order to allow those who follow a particular interest to find a partner in their enquiries and in their learning. Finally, there would be a reference service to 'educators-at-large', namely professionals and quasi-professionals and others with a freelance interest in helping to educate those who want their services.

There is nothing radical in these ideas nor is there anything radical about the specific components of the web. If, however, the de-schoolers truly represent the most radical of education's current critics, it should be of interest to work out how the four strands match with present-day practices and ideas.

In particular it would be of interest to compare the alternatives to school which the de-schoolers recommend with those who speak, less radically perhaps, for other alternatives – and notably for the idea of Free Schools. The latter are looked down upon by de-schoolers, who seem to feel that they represent a not very well-thought-out answer to the realisation that schools nowadays pose new social problems. The curricula of Free Schools are likened to the up-dated liturgies and masses which some Catholic bishops permitted (or encouraged) after the last Vatican Council: folk and rock music came to the clerical fore.

For their own part, however, the advocates of alternative schooling who do not go as far as Illich commend principles which are very near to his. One recommendation for alternatives, for instance (from Royston Lambert), starts from the recognition of straightforward principles which have underlain the progressivist tradition of English education in this century. These principles include the recognition that a child is a distinct individual whose whole development is a matter of concern for education, that individuals should be allowed to develop at their own pace, that children should be encouraged to acquire their own values in an open society and that children, too, have rights and responsibilities as moral agents.

In a way comparable to that of Illich the recommendation for action is equally unsurprising: young people need support and guidance but not necessarily from teachers, they need a base which is different from their home and which yet is not school, they need to develop by interaction in groups with other young people – and the list continues.

The outcrops of progressivism within English education have been well-charted; they have made an impact on individual teachers and on institutions. Influence has dwindled but the message has lingered on. As the original progressivists disappear into the distance of history, newcomers should take their place. It is about their stature that we are uncertain: are we to assume that the Free School of Liverpool is a successor to A. S. Neill and are we to accept that sundry attempts at providing other alternative forms will follow the steps of Rudolf Steiner?

The British system since 1902 has been able to make sense of a handful of progressive thinkers and of brilliant individual teachers who were forceful enough to make a clear impact on the education of the mass of children. Performers of that quality have never been numerous; in the nature of things they never *can* be numerous. But the way in which the educational system is managed seems to indicate that reform, however radical, can be coped with if its points of application are few in number and if the quality of the reform is such as to allow it to be taken seriously. What is inconceivable at this stage is that there should be a mass reform which would extensively and deeply affect the nature of present day education. We can stand so much change but not too much. To go too far, too fast, and too widely would be unacceptable to teachers and to parents, to authorities, and in the end to pupils and students themselves.

If one is to attempt to place the movement towards de-schooling and alternative schooling in some context we are bound to look at its intention. If people are saying that conventional education will no longer suffice, then reformers within the conventional system have been saying this for some time too. The Schools Council says it in one way, the Free School of Liverpool says it in another. The Nuffield Foundation takes steps to ensure that reform shall have an impact backed by money, the de-schoolers make sure that the impact of their message should be supported largely – and perhaps only – by a depth of feeling. But if money is the thing which creates power within education (as within any other system of publicly administered activity), then the de-schooling movement can attract sympathisers and supporters but it can make little difference. It is unlikely that, apart from isolated instances of support, it can have a very direct or extensive effect on resources. However, if de-schoolers make their message sufficiently plain, it is certain that there will be many who will be at least attracted to the possibilities of a more exciting pattern of change than that which depends simply upon the renewal of mundane affairs such as examinations.

Alternative forms of schooling are more likely to prove manageable within the independent sector than – at least in the first place – in the state sector of education. In the private sector alternative schooling can be handled in much the same way as progressive schooling was handled in the 1930s and 1940s. It is possible, however, that the effects of alternatives will be quicker in the next two decades than they have been in the past. The period in which either the diffusion or the implementation of a particular change is felt within schools at large is becoming briefer. Those who manage state systems of education, whether these are local education authorities or individual schools, must acknowledge that there will be those who – now as students and later as teachers and, later still, as parents, voters, rate-payers, and electors in a national scene – will wish to make their voices heard.

Unless the managers of change accept that the authority as well as the basis of the present system can be deeply and effectively challenged, there is the risk that we could delude ourselves into thinking that the improvements which are brought about piecemeal, slowly, with repute, and with a considerable degree of professional support will be all-sufficient; but these will not be enough in the end.

Summary

The management of change is neither clean nor self-contained. There are no magic rules and there are no formulae which are all-encompassing. The problems which confront education are diverse not only in their nature and quality but also in their points of origin. We cannot simply regard the management of innovation or of development as a matter of looking in one direction, of accepting national patterns of change, or of regarding problems of local implementation as falling neatly within one total format.

The differences between change and development are clear. The management of those less definable activities which fall within the overall definition of change can be sub-divided into what we might describe as movements, as planned changes and as fashions. Examples of each of these categories have been examined and the principal differences between the way in which change can be handled may be seen to be that gradual, reasonable and self-explanatory movements of ideas attract ready support and require no drastic action on the part of the manager.

The mixture, on the other hand, of planned change and the movement of ideas is something which is less certain in its handling. Team teaching, interdisciplinary projects – these are examples of the kind of conception which have a more immediate appeal for the practitioner. But at the same time they carry with them some doubt as to their total applicability as well as some reservation in the degree to which what were originally other countries' ideas can be applied to the culture of education in Britain. The management, therefore, of a hybrid breed of novelties requires a sensitivity not only to what happens in English education, to the sensibilities and levels of readiness which exist amongst English teachers but also to the origins which ideas such as these have within social, political and pedagogic systems overseas.

Anyone who is deeply interested in education can understand the nature of people's concerns when they wish to challenge the whole basis of an existing way of doing things. Revolutions of thought have to be extremely well-substantiated – but they also have to have a ready hearing if they are to catch on quickly. The likelihood is that the more revolutionary ideas with which the manager of an educational system is at present faced (and these may include questions of alternative schooling) have insufficient substance to create any real demand for accommodation *within* the system.

To manage change which has origins as diffuse, as revolutionary, as sincere and as undefined as those who advocate de-schooling presents either an enormous problem or no problem at all. It seems unlikely that there is a middle way for the manager. In terms of the microcosm of the school those who have to cope with mass truancy, with student protest, with the preference to attend rallies rather than lessons – within this smaller context of education the manager, the Head, the senior teacher (whoever it may be) is faced with manageable problems. There are precedents, regulations, rules and statutes.

In contrast, it is those who have responsibility for the quality of the system as a whole who will ultimately be faced with larger questions about the meaning and value attached to their present way of doing things. It is unlikely that a book about the management of change or about the way in which development can be handled within or outside existing systems can offer help. Nevertheless the simple message ought to be clear. Even if we do not take revolutionary ideas too seriously, we should be aware that revolution is in the air, that it is international in its origins and that what happens abroad may happen in Britain within two decades. We should at least try to be ready to learn lessons which other people are at present being taught.

10 Is there a future for curriculum development?

Curriculum development is meant to produce change. It can be planned and some of its outcomes can be foreseen. But it differs from other kinds of development in rather obvious ways: for instance, it differs in scale and style from an exercise such as that, for example, of the wing form of, for instance, a supersonic aeroplane.

A new aircraft with specific new potentials presents problems which can be defined. Designs which are meant to solve clear problems are wrought in a manner which depends upon the designer knowing exactly what he is aiming at. Successful design means that the designer can meet all the problems with which he is faced. If he falls short of total success those who are dependent upon him know whether they have to modify other components of the aeroplane. Because so many highly important other things depend on it, the development of a good wing design is something which has to be circumscribed. It is extremely difficult, no doubt, to meet all requirements. Doubtless, too, high skill and great persistence are essential in the whole process of design. The layman would expect no variable to be left to chance; he would not expect luck or hunch to enter into the designer's success.

By contrast there is a difference in the development of ideas and in the impetus towards other discoveries in fields where the demands of technical design are not dominant. For example, the account of the discovery of DNA describes it as a mixture of hunch, hard work, laborious and patient analysis and calculation. Here the development of an idea depended, as in the world of experimental engineering, on success in research. It was known that an idea which could change the face of a large area of science might be the outcome. But unlike the approach to engineering design, the attempt to *discover* something represents a process which is less formal, shapely and definable.

By contrast with the excitements of high level design and discovery in expensive and prestigious fields where competition (whether between commercial interests or Nobel prizewinners) is keen, changes in education differ both in type and in degree. Changes are not a matter of design, are not activities to which a known end can be hoped for, nor are they matters of startling and radical discovery which are likely to change men's view of the world at large.

Education changes slowly, shapelessly and in a way which is more or less uncontrolled. The management of it is not a matter of dealing with hard fact, clear aim, established policies, brilliant scientific rivalry, nor is it something which often receives acclamation within the public domain at large.

The teacher and the system

If education improves, develops, changes or differs in any way from decade to decade, it is because particular people in particular fields have had the patience, good fortune, insight and good experience which is necessary to make them credible when they wish to commend something new to other people.

Although there are risks in taking too easy a line in simplifying the description of how change occurs in the nebulous business of education, there is little point in relying too much upon abstractions, hypotheses or models. These are likely too often to be thought of as phantoms.

The *idea* of education is not something which those who are in it often appear to think about. Nor do those in the job often think or talk abstractly about the educational process. More often, they regard themselves as part of a system or of a service. They work in a known framework of public activity.

The majority of teachers and developers are those who (apart from the few who work in university schools of education) earn their living in the daily business of teaching children. Most of these work in local education authorities. They work within the scope of statute and the principal statute indirectly requires that if you work in any one sector of public education you should at least be aware that there are other parts – and that they have their own importance.

The Education Acts which govern England and Wales affect the curriculum of children from below the age of five to young people of about the age of eighteen. There are definable segments within this age range and teachers have loyalties, experiences and preferred ideas in each sub-division.

Curriculum development at its most practical is concerned with an education service which offers schooling to a carefully defined range of pupils. The definition of the age and type of student makes things workable. It also means that when those who manage curriculum development wish to appeal to teachers who are responsible for providing education in its most direct form in classrooms, they have to be aware of the particular audience to whom they speak. Teachers are part of a publicly controlled system: their loyalty, when change is mooted, is to principles of professionalism rather than simply to ideals of better learning.

Thus, in the context of a statutory service the development of curriculum is a matter of manageable and definable things or persons. The persons are parents, teachers and children. Curriculum development will not work unless those who are parents of children in schools present sufficient support and understanding at home for the work of schools to have some bite. Curriculum development will not work if teachers are not trained to expect that their role will change, that their task will need overhauling every five years or so, or that their outlook on what is meant by professionalism will be subject to both informed and unenlightened influences during the entire period of their working life.

Children matter because curriculum in the end is intended to ensure that they become better people than those who were educated before them. If curriculum is simply meant to provide a repetition, generation by generation, of comparable attitudes, similar expectations and identical capacities to fulfil roles within the industrial or social world, then the idea of development need not be raised in any way. But the larger system of social and economic expectation in which the education service is placed is further away from the teacher in the classroom. His relationship to the bigger system is indirect.

Apart from people, the manageable parts of the curriculum deals also with resources. Money matters because it can provide better education both initially and in terms of in-service training for teachers. Money matters, too, because it can provide better buildings in which children may carry out their learning and, also, that essential part of the process of curriculum development, namely the provision of a physically identifiable teachers' centre. Money also matters because it can buy materials which directly affect children's ways of learning. But the financial system behind education is something to which the teacher is only indirectly connected.

The future of the system

If the future of curriculum development is confined to quite simple definitions of practical matters affecting people and resources, the outlook may appear fairly bleak. People can be changed (even if we could skilfully use the ill-judged idea of social engineering) only slowly. Resources, too, can be increased year by year only in a very marginal way. The manager has little room for manoeuvre. There is little that he can quickly add to his repertoire and there is not much that he can expect by way of greater direct assistance from those who can change the professional preparation of teachers. If, therefore, he is to manage anything it has to be confined to matters of attitude. Yet we know that to speak about attitude-change as though it were something which in itself were concise, definable, manageable or capable of being planned – that this is an illusion.

The education service provides the bare bones around which to create the body of curriculum. There is ample room for despair about the speed of change, about the depth of its effect and about the measure to which it is possible to avoid abuse of that which is new. Yet, as in all public activities, it is unreal to expect that things can be neat and tidy. Curriculum is dependent upon so many variable factors and upon so many differences of experience, training and attitude that management faces an impossible task within the conventional description of the word.

But this does not mean that we should be satisfied merely to wring our hands. Management of any human activity which depends upon the way in which people value certain attitudes and certain types of behaviour is bound to depend to some extent upon hieratic influences, upon preaching and upon a certain degree of spiritual sleight of hand. Thus, the manager of curriculum development has to be aware not only of the various ways in which people can do things systematically within his own field but, also, he has to remember the weight of human experience. He has to have sense, maturity, an awareness of the history of educational change, and above all he has to have patience and a faith in people. The manager has to know that it is unreal to expect rapid change or to assume that people will take on fresh attitudes of value overnight. He also has to know that to stand back – aghast, apathetic and lethargic – will achieve nothing. He has to balance enthusiasm with commonsense, knowledge with zeal, experience with hope.

To place emphasis on the manager's personal skill is inevitable. But if we are to describe his skills, we can only talk about them in the way in which we now know them. Will a different system of education make other demands?

We have already seen that radical differences of the type related to de-schooling are unlikely to have a direct or deep effect on the management of curriculum development. But if other changes come about within the education service itself, the story would be different.

If local government reorganisation places rich and poor local education authorities together, money will have to be spent for a decade in reducing disparities and in trying to equalise basic items such as capitation allowances, grants to pupils and expenditure on school apparatus, equipment and books. If the spending of money has to be made consistent in the process of creating uniformity where it previously did not exist, the expansion, improvement and development of education services cannot be afforded.

Money spent on education can usually promote improvement in five spheres. These are, firstly, capital expenditure on new developments such as nursery education and capital expenditure on enlargements of a service, such as in further education and in higher education. Secondly, the improvement of staffing ratio. This can take one of three forms: the simple reduction in the number of pupils per teacher in all classes or the addition of new appointments to meet particular needs (such as the appointment of counsellors or of additional compensatory teachers for infant children) or the deliberate expansion of subject choices through the appointment of more staff than usual in, for instance, small comprehensive schools. Thirdly, more money can be spent on providing substitute teachers in order to replace those who attend training courses. Fourth, more money can be spent on books, apparatus and equipment. Fifth, the direct expansion either of in-service training or in the size of a local authority's advisory service can also eat up money.

Of these five, it is only capital expenditure on buildings which does not have a direct effect on curriculum improvement. There is admittedly an indirect effect which is noticeable but the other categories matter more to individual schools; and it is in these categories that the reorganisation of local government and the need to unify educational policies (and their financial consequences) will be most likely to lead to a standstill.

The future system of education in England and Wales will, then, not radically change. But financial – and hence human – resources will be limited. Development usually means expansion; expansion will be stopped. Curriculum development is not likely, in the next ten years of the local education system, to flourish.

If things look black at the local level, will there be a compensating increase in expenditure and activity at national level? The principal agencies for national change in England and Wales are the Department of Education and Science, whose effect on curriculum is subtle but not widespread, the Schools Council, whose credibility as well as its resources may now be reaching a limit, and the National Foundation for Educational Research, whose budget, effect and scope for action is, again, very limited. For money, the DES depends on the Treasury directly; the Schools Council and the NFER depend heavily on local authority grants. Local authority grants are indirectly affected by annual rate support grants – which again depend upon the Treasury and upon central government policy for priority within its total domestic expenditure.

Nationally, then, the scene is cheerless. But another source of aid may be that of the universities: they depend through the University Grants Committee upon the Treasury, and increasingly higher education's spending is monitored by the Secretary of State for Education and Science. However, within the budget of an university, is there likely to be much more spent within the next decade on education? The answer is probably no. With a few exceptions, Institutes of Education tend to be poor relations within the university world. And if more money is spent on education it is likely to be devoted to increasing the number of graduate teachers or to producing what was, at least in the early days after the 1972 White Paper, the more or less unknown entity who might emerge from courses for the Diploma of Higher Education. As the effect of polytechnics and the Council for National Academic Awards are increasingly felt on the provision of B.Ed. courses and as the Open University, too, increases the opportunities which teachers can find to gain a graduate qualification, the competition against Institutes of Education, Schools of Education, and colleges of education will grow more fierce. It would be unreasonable to think that in-service training or curriculum development can benefit from any greatly increased expenditure. The 1972 White Paper contained exhortations but, in this sphere at least, added no promise of additional financial support.

The immediate future of educational spending seems, then, to make it impossible to be optimistic about curriculum. The heyday of interest may be over – certainly insofar as interest attracted money in late 1960s and early 1970s. But with luck, there will be no reduction in the amount of money which already aids curriculum work in several different ways. And questions about the future then come down to alternative ways of spending money.

Choices about basic resources

The management of curriculum development assumes that changing the teacher is desirable and that progressively more change is required amongst more teachers.

The assumption has its dangers. It takes for granted the right of some to know better than others, of the employer to expect a chosen difference in behaviour in his employee, of the expert to be given a hearing (and belief) from those who are supposedly less expert.

The assumption, too, is often argued about as though the demands on education were to be cumulative. It is from this kind of reasoning that those exhortations begin which urge the acceleration of in-service training: what is outdated in this period will be primitive by comparison in five years time.

There is no inevitability about the progress of curriculum development nor is there inevitability about the way in which teachers may be expected to alter what they do. Teaching is a profession in which much depends, as in all professions, on the integrity and energy of the individual member.

If a teacher knows that there are new ideas afoot, if he realises that the method, content, purpose and style of teaching is under review, he will act unprofessionally if he does not take his own steps to find out and think about what is new and then act – and whether he acts in acceptance or rejection matters less than that he should have devoted honest thought to the problem. Hence, the basis of curriculum development has to be trust that the teacher knows where he needs help. He may only need slight stimulus or some added confidence; he may need only a little fresh information before setting off on his own quest.

If trust rather than a thinly veiled moral compulsion were the basis of curriculum development, despair about resources might be avoided. The less teachers are relied upon to find their own professional salvation and to mend their own fences, the greater will be the demand for more training, more trainers, more time, more money, more development projects and more research. The less discriminate these demands, the more endless will the job of development seem.

In a rich country curriculum development, educational reform and the overall improvement of schooling can eat up any amount of energy, skill and money. If, however, the statement of problems were sufficient, if teachers were trained and expected to see a continuing responsibility to monitor their professional performance and the efficiency of their professional equipment, they would find their own method of self-renewal. Resources would then cease to go in one direction: the emphasis on retraining which starts from sources outside the teacher himself would diminish.

Resources, in an alternative way, would then be used to stimulate and to interest teachers, to provide a variety of non-training aids and to provide a milieu in which the person's own sense of responsibility would be a paramount force. Instead of the continual repetition of one type of answer (that of formalised in-service training), the creation could begin of what has sometimes been called a learning community.

The shape and focus of such a community would change from time to time. The most essential part would shift from being sometimes within a school to a college of education, to a teachers' centre, to a research unit, to a library – or to discussion and to private reading on the part of the teacher himself. The provision of money for the organisation of development and training would pay less attention to fixed systems than to the possibility of catching needs, teachers' readiness, inclinations, – and time and energy – at the moment when these could best be directed to one purpose.

If a future pattern of development could reflect more of the sense of chance by which we usually learn, review and reform any part of our professional way of life, there would not be the need to look ahead to steadily mounting costs and to the steady exhaustion of sources of leadership. Leadership would matter less than stimulus and inspiration – and these could come from a number of different directions.

If responsibility can be exercised at the level at which people are pricked by their own consciences, if a movement forward is to depend upon individual insight, and if we can in the end accept the fact that curriculum development is unmanageable in the sense of our *current* (and brief) tradition of management, then it virtually ceases to be a public activity.

Summary

Curriculum development has to be something which means a great deal to the teacher. It has to offer hope to those who have faith in the total effects of education and it also has to be something which does not pose questions about extremes of unreality. Those who have a responsibility for curriculum development have to know the limits of change. They have to see what it is that change requires of people and of financial resources.

In addition, curriculum and the definition of its aims has an increasing appeal to philosophers. Those who feel that educational objectives are too arbitrarily and perhaps bizarrely described, codified and analysed urge the power of clear language, good thinking and rigorous questioning. But will philosophers (empirical and pragmatic, or metaphysical and somewhat mystic) help very much in managing future development? It seems likely that their message about clear and simple thinking will, in the end, get through. But their demand for rigour, their scorn for the way in which teachers are allowed to stipulate rather than argue about their aims – the challenge here is unlikely to make much effect.

The development of education may be so particular to the individual teacher and so deeply coloured by the style of a single school that management can in turn only have significance in highly specific circumstances. If this is so it means that curriculum change is a long way away from abstractions which centre upon the control of knowledge or upon the economics of the acquisition and use of knowledge. Curriculum development is, in brief, at such a rudimentary stage of life that to attempt to apply refined and sophisticated modes of thinking to its management is premature.

Time may show that curriculum and the extension of reform within it is likely to be a permanent concern for those in education. At present we can only assume that this will be so. But the assumption is too tenuous to support too heavy a structure of planning and rationalisation.

Books and Sources

AUTHOR'S NOTE
This book attempts to cover a large subject in a few pages. The ideas and arguments in it have often taken their starting-point from the stimulus, information and scholarship of other writers.

Most of the sources are listed here. Not all are easily accessible; to help anyone who wishes to read further without too much special effort, some books and articles are marked with an asterisk.

*Allen, B. (ed.), *Headship in the 1970s*. Oxford, Basil Blackwell, 1968.
Barr, R. M. (ed.), *Curriculum innovation in practice*. Edgehill College of Education, 1969.
Bassett, G. W., *Innovation in primary education*. London, John Wiley, 1970.
Beauchamp, G. A. & K. E., *Comparative analysis of curriculum systems*. Wilmette, Ill., The Kagg Press, 1967.
Becker, H. S., Geer, B. & Hughes, E. C., *Making the grade*. New York, John Wiley, 1968.
Bell, R. (ed.), *Thinking about the curriculum*. Bletchley, The Open University Press, 1971.
*Bennis, W., Benne, K. & Chin, R. (edd.), *The planning of change*. New York, Holt Rinehart & Winston, 1969.
Bishop, A. S., *The rise of a central authority for English education*. London, Cambridge University Press, 1971.
Black Papers 1, 2, and 3, see Critical Quarterly Society.
Blacksell, J. E., see Devon County Council, *The Head in the Secondary School*, 1969.
Board of Education, *Curriculum and examinations in secondary schools* (The Norwood Report). London, His Majesty's Stationery Office, 1943.
Handbook of suggestions for the consideration of teachers and others concerned in the work of public elementary schools. London, His Majesty's Stationery Office, 1937.
Report of the Consultative Committee on Examinations in Secondary Schools, Cd. 6004, 1911, quoted in Appendix I of *Secondary Schools Examinations*, Ministry of Education, 1958.
Report of the Consultative Committee on psychological tests of educable capacity and their possible use in the public system of education. London, His Majesty's Stationery Office, 1924.
Report of the Consultative Committee on the Primary School (Hadow Report, 1931). London, His Majesty's Stationery Office, 1931.
Report of the Consultative Committee on Secondary Education (Spens Report). London, His Majesty's Stationery Office, 1938.
The Education of the Adolescent (Hadow Report, 1926). London, His Majesty's Stationery Office, 1926.

Bruner, J. S., *The process of education*. Harvard, The University Press, 1960.
The relevance of education. London, George Allen & Unwin, 1972.
The relevance of skill or the skill of relevance. London, Encyclopaedia Britannica, 1970.
**Towards a theory of instruction*. Cambridge, Mass., Harvard University Press, 1966.
Bryce Report (*Report of the Royal Commission on Secondary Education*), 1895, see Maclure, J. S., *Educational Documents*.
Burns, T. & Stalker, J., *Management of innovation*. London, Tavistock Publications, 1961.
*Callahan, R. E., *Education and the cult of efficiency*. Chicago, University of Chicago Press, 1962.
Cane, B., *In-service training*, Occasional Publications Series No. 22. Slough, National Foundation for Educational Research, 1969.
Carlson, R. O., *The adoption of educational innovations*. Eugene, Center for the Advanced Study of Educational Administration, 1965.
Cave, R. G., *An introduction to curriculum development*. London, Ward Lock Educational, 1971.
Centre for Educational Research and Innovation, *The nature of the curriculum for the eighties and onwards*. Paris, Organisation for Economic Co-operation and Development, 1972.
Civil Service: Report of the Committee 1966-68, London, Cd. 3638, Her Majesty's Stationery Office, 1968 (Fulton Report).
Cook, A. & Mack, H., *The headteacher's role*. London, Macmillan, 1971.
Corbett, A., *Innovation in education: England*. Paris, OECD, Centre for Educational Research and Innovation, 1971.
*Cosin, B., Dale, I., Esland, G. & Swift, D., *School and society: a sociological reader*. London, Routledge & Kegan Paul, 1971.
Critical Quarterly Society: *Fight for Education*, 1969;
The Crisis in Education, 1969:
Black Paper 3, 1970;
London, Critical Quarterly Society.
Curriculum Study Group, see Ministry of Education, *Education in 1963*, pp. 25-6.
Davies, I. K., *The management of learning*. London, McGraw Hill, 1971.
Davies, T. I., *School Organisation*. London, Pergamon Press, 1969.
Department of Education & Science, *Children and their Primary Schools* (Plowden Report). A report of the Central Advisory Council for Education (England). London, Her Majesty's Stationery Office, 1967.
Educational Pamphlet No. 21: *The School Library*. London, Her Majesty's Stationery Office, 1967.
Educational Pamphlet No. 56: *Commercial Studies in Schools*. London, Her Majesty's Stationery Office, 1970.
Educational Priority Volume 1: EPA Problems and Policies (Halsey Report). London, Her Majesty's Stationery Office, 1972.
Education Survey No. 2: *Drama*. London, Her Majesty's Stationery Office, 1967.
Primary Education in Wales, Central Advisory Council for Education (Wales) (Gittins Report). London, Her Majesty's Stationery Office, 1967.
Statistics of Education, Special Series No. 2: *Survey of in-service training for teachers, 1967*. London, Her Majesty's Stationery Office, 1970.
Teacher Education and Training: a report by a committee of inquiry (James Report). London, Her Majesty's Stationery Office, 1972.
Devon County Council, *Leadership in Primary Schools*. Exeter, Devon County Council, Education Department, 1969.

BOOKS AND SOURCES

The Head in the Secondary School. Exeter, Devon County Council, Education Department, 1969.
Education, A Framework for Expansion, Cmnd 5174 (1972 White Paper). London, Her Majesty's Stationery Office, 1972.
Enquiry 1, see Morton Williams, R.
Evans, P., *see* Devon County Council, *Leadership in Primary Schools.*
Examinations in Public Elementary Schools: the report of the Enquiry undertaken by the Joint Advisory Committee of the Association of Education Committees and the National Union of Teachers into Examinations for Pupils in Public Elementary Schools. London, Education and The Schoolmaster, 1930.
Fantini, M. & Weinstein, G., *The disadvantaged challenge to education.* New York, Harper & Row, 1968.
Freeman, J., *Team teaching in Britain.* London, Ward Lock, 1969.
Fulton Report, *see* Civil Service, Report of Committee, 1966-68.
Gardner, J. W., *Excellence: can we be equal and excellent too?* New York, Harper & Row, 1961.
**Self-renewal: the individual and the innovative society.* New York, Harper & Row, 1963.
*Gibb, C. A. (ed.), *Leadership.* London, Penguin Books, 1969.
Gittins Report, *see* Department of Education & Science, *Primary Education in Wales.*
Glasser, W., *Schools without failure.* New York, Harper & Row, 1969.
Glatter, R., *Management development for the education profession.* London, George Harrap, 1972.
Goffman, E., *Strategic interaction.* Oxford, Basil Blackwell, 1970.
Goodlad, J. I., *School, curriculum, and the individual.* Waltham, Mass., Blaisdell Publishing Company, 1966.
Goodman, P., *Compulsory miseducation.* London, Penguin Books, 1971.
Grobman, H., *Developmental curriculum projects: decision points and processes.* New York, F. E. Peacock Publishers Inc., 1970.
Gross, N., Giacquinta, J. B. & Bernstein, M., *Implementing organisational innovations.* New York, Harper & Row, 1971.
*Gross, R. & Gross, B. (edd.), *Radical school reform.* London, Victor Gollancz, 1971.
Hadow Report 1926, *see* Board of Education, *The Education of the Adolescent.*
Hadow Report 1931, *see* Board of Education, *Report of the Consultative Committee on the Primary School.*
Halpin, A. W., *Theory and research in educational administration.* New York, Macmillan, 1966.
Halsey, A. H., Floud, J. & Anderson, C. A., *Education, economy and society.* London, Collier Macmillan, 1961.
Halsey, A. H. (ed.), *Trends in British society since 1900.* London, Macmillan, 1972.
Hannam, C., Smyth, P. & Stephenson, N., *Young teachers and reluctant learners.* London, Penguin Books, 1971.
Hartog, P. & Rhodes, E. C., *Examination of examinations.* London, Macmillan, 1935.
Henry, J., *Essays on education.* London, Penguin Books, 1971.
Hirst, P. H. & Peters, R. S., *The logic of education.* London, Routledge & Kegan Paul, 1970.
*Hooper, R., *The curriculum: context, design and development.* Edinburgh, Oliver & Boyd, 1971.
Hoyle, E., 'How does the curriculum change?' in *Journal of Curriculum Studies,* vol. 1, Nos. 1 & 2. London, Collins, 1969.
*Hoyle, E. & Bell, R. (edd.), *Problems of curriculum innovation, I & II.* Bletchley, The Open University Press, 1972.

Humanities Project: an introduction. London, Heinemann Educational Books Limited, 1970.

Illich, I. D., *Deschooling society.* London, Calder & Boyars, 1971.

Isaacs, S., *Social development in young children: a study of beginnings.* London, Routledge, 1933.

The children we teach. London, University of London Press, 1932.

Jackson, P. S., *Life in classrooms.* New York, Holt Rinehart & Winston, 1968.

James, C., *Young lives at stake: a reappraisal of secondary schools.* London, Collins, 1968

James Report, *see* Department of Education & Science, *Teacher education and training 1972.*

Jenkins, D., Pring, R. & Harris, A. (edd.), *Curriculum philosophy and design.* Bletchley, The Open University Press, 1972.

Johnston, D. J., *Teachers' in-service education.* Oxford, Pergamon Press, 1971.

Kerr, J. F. (ed.), *Changing the curriculum.* London, University of London Press, 1968.

Koerner, J. D., *Reform in education.* London, Weidenfeld & Nicolson, 1968.

Lacey, W. D., Medd, D. L., Burrows, L. J., Pearson, E., *The evolving school,* in *Trends in Education No. 2.* London, Her Majesty's Stationery Office, 1966.

Lambert, R., *Alternatives to school.* Exeter, University of Exeter, 1972.

Maclure, J. S., *Curriculum innovation in practice.* London, Her Majesty's Stationery Office, 1968.

**Educational Documents: England and Wales, 1816-1968.* London, Methuen Education, 1969.

McClelland, D. C., *The achieving society.* Princeton, Van Nostrand Co. Inc., 1961

*McClure, R. M. (ed.), *The curriculum: retrospect and prospect.* Chicago, Ill., University of Chicago Press, 1971.

McNair Report: *Report of a Committee appointed by the President of the Board of Education to consider the Supply, Recruitment, and Training of Teachers and Youth Leaders.* London, His Majesty's Stationery Office, 1944.

Marland, M., *Head of department: leading a department in a comprehensive school.* London, Heinemann, 1971.

Mason, E., *Collaborative learning.* London, Ward Lock Educational, 1970.

Martin, W. T. (ed.), *Curriculum improvement and innovation: a partnership of students, school teachers and research scholars.* Cambridge, Mass., Robert Bentley Inc., 1966.

Medd, D. L., *Designing for people,* in *Trends in Education No. 15.* London, Her Majesty's Stationery Office, 1969.

Merritt, J. & Harris, A. (edd.), *Curriculum design and implementation.* Bletchley, The Open University Press, 1972.

Miles, M. B. (ed.), *Innovation in Education.* New York, Teachers College Press, Columbia, 1964.

Ministry of Education, *Education in 1963.* London, Her Majesty's Stationery Office, 1964.

Half our future. A report of the Central Advisory Council for Education (England) (Newsom Report). London, Her Majesty's Stationery Office, 1963.

Secondary Schools Examinations other than the GCE: Report of a Committee appointed by the Secondary Schools Examinations Council July 1958. London, Her Majesty's Stationery Office, 1960.

The scope and standards of the Certificate of Secondary Education: the Seventh Report of the Secondary Schools Examinations Council. London, Her Majesty's Stationery Office, 1963.

Ministry of Housing & Local Government, *People and planning* (Skeffington Report). London, Her Majesty's Stationery Office, 1969.

Montgomery, R. J., *Examinations: an account of their evolution as administrative devices in England.* London, Longmans, 1965.
Morrell, D. H., *Education and change.* London, Joseph Payne Memorial Lectures, College of Preceptors, 1966.
*Morton-Williams, R. & Finch, S., Schools Council *Enquiry 1: Young School Leavers.* London, Her Majesty's Stationery Office, 1968.
Musgrove, F., *Patterns of power and authority in English education.* London, Methuen, 1971.
Musgrove, R. & Taylor, P. H., *Society and the teacher's role.* London, Routledge & Kegan Paul, 1969.
National Education Association, *Rational planning in curriculum and instruction.* Washington D.C., National Education Association of the United States, 1967.
Newcastle Commission (*Report of the Commissioners Appointed to Inquire into the State of Popular Education in England*), 1861. See Maclure, J. S., *Educational Documents.*
Newsom Report, *see* Ministry of Education *Half Our Future,* 1963.
Nisbet, S. D., *Purpose in the curriculum.* London, University of London Press, 1957.
Norwood Report, *see* Board of Education, *Curriculum and Examinations in Secondary Schools,* 1943.
Ontario Institute for Studies in Education, *Emerging strategies and structures for educational change.* Ontario, Institute for Studies in Education, 1966.
Otty, N., *Learner teacher.* London, Penguin Books, 1972.
Owen, J. G., 'Administration of curriculum change', in Baron & Taylor (edd.), *Educational Administration and the Social Sciences.* London, The Athlone Press, 1969.
'Changing patterns of Canadian curriculum', in *Journal of Curriculum Studies,* vol. 2, no. 2. London, Collins, 1970.
'Comparative education, curriculum, and the serving teacher', in *Education for Teaching.* London, Spring 1971.
'Curriculum and teachers' centres: a progress report', in *Trends in Education,* Autumn 1972. London, Department of Education & Science, HMSO.
'Curriculum for the young school leaver', in *Educational Review,* vol. 21, no. 3. University of Birmingham, 1969.
'Curriculum innovation in the USSR', in *Journal of Curriculum Studies,* vol. 1, no. 3. London, Collins, 1969.
'Curriculum in West Germany', in *Education,* 28 February 1969. London, Councils & Education Press.
'Educational innovation: the human factor', in *Journal of Educational Administration and History,* vol. ii, no. 3. University of Leeds, 1970.
'Educational innovation: the role of teachers' centres in a decentralized system'. Paper prepared for research council of Deutscher Bildungsrat, Bonn, 1972.
'Lehrerzentren als Curriculumlaboratorien – eine kritische Beurteilung', in *Curriculumentwicklung in der diskussion.* Dusseldorf, Pädagogischer Verlag Schwann, 1972.
'Local education authorities and the improvement of curriculum', in Hoyle & Bell (edd.), *Problems of curriculum innovation, ii.* Bletchley, The Open University Press, 1972.
'Participation of teachers in curriculum development: experiences in teachers' centres'. Paper for Deutscher Bildungsrat, Bonn, 1972.
'School-centred patterns of support and resistance'. Conference paper, The Management of Change, Paris, OECD, Centre for Educational Research and Innovation, 1969.
'Strategies of curriculum innovation', in *Journal of Curriculum Studies,* vol. 1, no. 1. London, Collins, 1968.

BOOKS AND SOURCES

'Teachers' centres, their personnel and their place in the structure of education'. Conference paper: University of London, Institute of Education, 1971.

'Teacher education: local education authorities as providing bodies', in Taylor, W. (ed.), *Towards a Policy for the Education of Teachers*. London, Butterworth, 1969.

Pai, Y. & Myers, J. T., *Philosophic problems and education*. Philadelphia, J. B. Lippincott Company, 1967.

Palmer, R., *Space, time, and grouping*. London, Macmillan, 1971.

Payne, A., *The study of curriculum plans*. Washington D.C., National Education Association, 1969.

Peters, R. S. (ed.), *The concept of education*. London, Routledge & Kegan Paul, 1967.

Phenix, P. H., *Philosophy of Education*. New York, Holt Rinehart & Winston, 1958.

Plowden Report, *see* Department of Education & Science, *Children and their Primary Schools*.

Pugh, D. S., *Writers on organisations*. London, Hutchinson, 1964.

Raynor, J. & Grant, N. (edd.), *Patterns of curriculum*. Bletchley, The Open University Press, 1972.

Reimer, E., *School is dead*. London, Penguin Books, 1971.

Rich, J. M., *Conflict and decision: analysing educational issues*. New York, Harper & Row, 1972.

*Richardson, E., *The environment of learning*. London, Nelson, 1967.

*Richmond, W. K., *The School Curriculum*. London, Methuen, 1970.

Ridgway, L. & Lawton, I., *Family grouping in the primary school* (2nd edition). London, Ward Lock, 1968.

Rogers, E. M., *Diffusion of innovations*. New York, The Free Press of Glencoe, 1962.

Rosenthal, R. & Jacobson, L. F., *Pygmalion in the classroom*. New York, Holt Rinehart & Winston, 1968.

Rubin, L., *A study in the continuing education of teachers*. Santa Barbara, Center for Coordinated Education, University of California, 1970.

Sarason, S. B., *The culture of the school and the problem of change*. Boston, Allyn & Bacon Inc., 1971.

Scheffler, I., *Conditions of knowledge*. Glenview, Ill., Scott, Foresman & Co., 1965.

The language of education. Springfield, Ill., C. C. Thomas, 1960.

Schon, D. A., *Beyond the stable state*. London, Temple Smith, 1971.

Schools Council, *The New Curriculum*. London, Her Majesty's Stationery Office, 1967.

Working Paper No. 1: *Science for the Young School Leaver*. London, Her Majesty's Stationery Office, 1965.

*Working Paper No. 2: *Raising the School Leaving Age*. London, Her Majesty's Stationery Office, 1965.

Working Paper No. 3: *English: a programme for research and development in English teaching*. London, Her Majesty's Stationery Office, 1965.

*Working Paper No. 10: *Curriculum Development: teachers' groups and centres*. London, Her Majesty's Stationery Office, 1967.

Sixth Form Survey
vol. I: *Sixth Form Teachers and Pupils* (1970)
vol. II: *Students in full-time courses in Colleges of Further Education* (1970)
vol. III: *Sixth Form Leavers* (1971)
London, Books for Schools on behalf of Schools Council Publications.

*Schwab, J. J., *The practical: a language for curriculum*. Washington D.C., National Education Association, 1970

Seaman, P., Esland, G. & Cosin, B. (edd.), *Innovation and ideology*. Bletchley, The Open University Press, 1972.

Searle, J. R., *The Campus War*. London, Penguin Books, 1972.

Select Committee on Education & Science 1967-68, *H.M. Inspectorate*. London, Her Majesty's Stationery Office, 1968.

Shipman, M. & Raynor, J. (edd.), *Perspectives on the curriculum*. Bletchley, The Open University Press, 1972.

Silberman, C. E., *Crisis in the classroom*. New York, Random House, 1970.

Simon, B. (ed.), *The radical tradition in education in Britain*. London, Lawrence & Wishart, 1972.

Skeffington Report, see Ministry of Housing & Local Government, *People and Planning*.

Smith, B. O. & Ennis, R. H. (edd.), *Language and concepts in education: analytic study of educational ideas*. Chicago, Rand McNally & Co., 1961.

Smith, L. M. & Keith, P. M., *Anatomy of educational innovation*. New York, John Wiley & Sons Inc., 1971.

Snape, P., see Devon County Council, *The Head in the Secondary School*.

Soltis, J. F., *An introduction to the analysis of educational concepts*. Reading, Mass., Addison-Wesley, 1968.

Spens Report, see Board of Education, *Report of the Consultative Committee on Secondary Education, 1938*.

Stenhouse, L. A., 'The Humanities Curriculum Project', *Journal of Curriculum Studies*, vol. 1, no. 1. London, Collins, November 1968.

Sumner, R. & Warburton, F. W., *Achievement in secondary school: attitudes, personality and school success*. Slough, National Foundation for Educational Research, 1972.

Sussmann, L., *Innovation in education: United States*. Paris, OECD, Centre for Educational Research & Innovation, 1971.

Taba, H., *Curriculum development: theory and practice*. New York, Harcourt Brace & World Inc., 1962.

*Taylor, G. (ed.), *The teacher as manager*. London, Councils & Education Press, 1970.

Taylor, G. & Ayres, N., *Born and bred unequal*. London, Longman, 1969.

*Taylor, L. C., *Resources for learning*. London, Penguin Books, 1971.

*Taylor, P. H., *How teachers plan their courses*. Slough, National Foundation for Educational Research, 1970.

Thomas, R. M., Sands, L. B. & Brubaker, D. L., *Strategies for curriculum change*. Scranton, Penn., International textbook Company, 1968.

Toffler, A., *Future shock*. London, Bodley Head, 1970.

Townsend, H. E. R., see Department of Education & Science, *Statistics of Education, Special Series No. 2*.

Trump, J. Lloyd, *Images of the future: a new approach to secondary schools*. National Association of Secondary-School Principals, Commission of the experimental study of the utilization of the staff in the secondary school, 1959.

Tyler, L. L., *A selected guide to curriculum literature: an annotated bibliography*. Washington D.C., National Education Association, 1970.

*Tyler, R. W., *Basic principles of curriculum and instruction*. Chicago, University of Chicago Press, 1950.

UNESCO *World Survey of Education III: Secondary Education*. Paris, UNESCO, 1961.

Valentine, C. W., *The reliability of examinations: an enquiry, with special reference to the entrance examinations into secondary schools, the School Certificate and the award of scholarships at universities*. London, University of London Press, 1932.

Walton, J. (ed.), *Curriculum organisation and design*. London, Ward Lock Educational, 1971.

Warwick, D., *Team teaching*. London, University of London Press, 1971.

BOOKS AND SOURCES

White Paper 1972, *see Education, A Framework for Expansion*.
Whitfield, R. C., *Disciplines of the curriculum*. London, McGraw Hill, 1971.
*Wilson, J. B., *Philosophy and educational research*. Slough, National Foundation for Educational Research, 1972.
Wilson, P. S., *Interest and discipline in education*. London, Routledge & Kegan Paul, 1971.
*Wiseman, S. & Pidgeon, D., *Curriculum evaluation*. Slough, National Foundation for Educational Research, 1970.
Yates, A., *The organisation of schooling*. London, Routledge & Kegan Paul, 1971.
Young, M., *Innovation and research in education*. London, Routledge & Kegan Paul, 1964.
Young, M. F. D. (ed.), *Knowledge and control: new directions in the sociology of education*. London, Collier Macmillan, 1971.
Yudkin, M. (ed.), *General education*. London, Penguin Books, 1971.

Index

Accountability 7, 8, 11, 18, 20; chapter 3; 47, 82, 94, 147, 148, 152, 156
Achievement, and measurement 9, 13, 18, 19, 23, 30–1, 33–4
Adolescents, curricular needs 26f, 31, 64–6, 67
Advisory Centre for Education 119
Advisory services 36, 45, 46, 47, 89, 96, 101, 102–6, 110, 114, 116, 128, 129, 163
Age in schooling
 minimum leaving age 9, 16, 17, 27, 59–60, 64–6, 67
 transfer ages 15, 21, 31, 33, 34, 36, 71, 73, 118, 134
Area Training Organisations 44, 77, 103, 110, 111, 112, 115, 116
Arnold M. 57
Art, and aesthetic education 43, 44, 65
Assistant teachers, position of 12, 14, 15, 40–1, 53, 69–70, 82–3, 93, 98–9
Association of Education Committees 31
Association for Science Education 62, 112
Autonomy of teachers 9, 10, 19, 20, 22, 46, 53, 68, 69, 86–7, 93, 138

Banding of pupils 146
 and vertical grouping 132–7
 and non-streaming 145–7
Baron G. 118
Beloe Report 29
Bishop A.S. 7
Black Papers 147
Blacksell E. 70–1
Board of Education 9, 11, 12, 14, 18, 19, 26, 27, 28, 31
British Broadcasting Corporation 129, 130
Bruner J. 53

Bryce Report 11, 12, 14
Buildings 34, 47, 97, 117, 124–6, 138, 162

Canada 70, 85
Cane B. 115
Careers advice 65, 73
Careers Research Advisory Centre 119
Central Advisory Council for Education (England) 148
 Newsom Report (1963) 43, 59, 60, 64, 141, 144
 Plowden Report 33, 87, 88, 89, 91, 92, 138, 148, 149, 150
Central Advisory Council for Education (Wales)
 Gittins Report 33
Centre for Educational Research & Innovation 85
Certificate of Secondary Education 29, 30, 31, 35
Change and resistance chapter 6 passim; 98, 99
Charity Commission 12
Circular 286 (1913) 26
Civil Service, entrance requirement 25
Cockerton Judgement 12
Commercial studies 14, 16, 26, 43
Communication 6, 19, 69–70, 83, 84, 88, 89
Compensatory education 33, 66, 114, 162
Consultative Committees, reports
 Curriculum & Examinations in Secondary Schools (Norwood, 1943) 26, 29, 30
 Education of the Adolescent (Hadow, 1926) 31
 Examinations in Secondary Schools (1911) 27
 Primary Education (Hadow, 1931) 8, 15, 31, 32, 88

175

INDEX

Consultative Committees, reports— *cont.*
  Psychological Tests of Educable Capacity (1924)   9
  Secondary Education (Spens, 1938)   28
Continuity of learning   17, 73, 153
COSMOS   117, 118
Creative organisations   92, 93
Curriculum
  conformity   5, 6, 12, 19, 33, 68, 153, 154, 162
  public participation   20, 70, 149–50, 152, 155, 157
  language of reform   3, 38, 42, 46, 54, 81, 95
Curriculum Study Group   58

Davies I.   99
Davies T.I.   117
Day Trade Schools   14
Decentralisation of curriculum control   6, 7, 8, 9, 19, 63, 68, 86, 104
Decision-making   12, 14, 18, 20, 21, 58, 70, 80, 91, 93, 97–8, 116–18, 155
Definition of curriculum   3, 11, 16, 18, 20, 48, 89, 90
Delphi technique   55
Department of Education & Science   21, 42, 43, 44, 110, 111
De-schooling   151, 153–7
Design of curriculum   22, 29, 38, 39, 41, 45, 48–9, 53
Diffusion of reform   60, 61, 69–70
Drama   43, 44, 129

Eastern Europe   6
Education Acts   160
  1870   10
  1902   12, 14, 149
  1944   149
Educational technology   128
Eleven plus   33–6
English   61, 62, 65, 86
ETV   130
Evans P.   97
Examinations   23, 31; chapter 3 passim

Family grouping   132–7, 138, 139
Freeman J.   138, 140
Free Place system   14, 32
Free Schools   155, 156
French   96
Froebel   138

Fulton Report   45
Further Education   43, 71, 119, 162

General Certificate of Education   29, 30, 33, 34
General studies   35
Girls' education   25, 26
Gittins Report   33
Government Social Survey, *Enquiry 1*   42, 115
Grading   8, 9, 10, 15, 32, 73, 133, 136, 145–7
Grants from Central Government   7, 8, 11, 162, 163, 164
Grubb Institute   119
Guidance for teachers   14, 15, 18, 19, 21, 42–3, 44–8, 91

Hadow Report, 1926   31
Hadow Report, 1931   8, 15, 31, 32, 88
Hartog P. & Rhodes E.C.   31
Heads of departments in secondary schools   93, 96, 145
Head Teachers   44, 45, 79, 81, 82, 96, 97, 98, 99, 116–18, 120, 137, 146
Higher Elementary Schools   14
Higher Grade Board Schools   14
Higher School Certificate   28, 30
Hirst P.   90
Humanities Curriculum Project   35, 83, 145

Illich I.D.   154, 155
Individualised learning   22, 41, 127, 138, 139
Infant children   9, 15, 18, 36, 60, 87, 96, 124, 134, 162
Initial Teaching Alphabet   62
Inner London Education Authority   118
In-service training   41, 44, 73, 74–6
Inspectors   33, 36, 42, 44, 45, 46, 47, 57, 85, 86, 101, 102–6, 110, 111, 114, 115, 116
Institutes of Education   21, 63, 110, 114, 116, 163
  Area Training Organisations   44, 77, 103, 111, 112
Integrated day   136, 138, 139
Integrated studies   35, 65, 137, 140–5, 157
Interdisciplinary Enquiry   140
Isaacs S.   132, 136

INDEX

James C. 140
James Report 108–9
Junior Technical Schools 14

Kerr J. 90

Lambert R. 155
Local Education Authorities 9, 10, 12, 14, 16, 18, 19, 21, 44, 101, 102, 103, 104, 105, 106, 110–11, 113, 114, 116, 118, 152, 163
Local government reform 105, 148, 149, 152, 162
London School Board 12

McNair Report 77
Managers and governors of schools 9, 10, 149, 150, 151, 152
Mathematics 15, 18, 65, 96, 97–8
Medd D. 124
Micro-teaching 120–4, 126
Middle years of schooling 73, 114, 118, 134
Moral education 6, 7, 20, 60, 64, 153
Morrell D.H. 58
Musgrove F. 90
Music 45, 129

National Association for the Teaching of English 62, 112
National comparisons 6, 57, 58, 85, 158
National Foundation for Educational Research 115, 163
National Union of Teachers 31, 66, 69, 70, 109, 113, 116
Neill A.S. 156
Newcastle Commission 8, 9
Newsom Report (1963) 43, 59, 60, 64, 141, 144
New teachers 116, 126
Non-streaming 33, 137, 145–7
Northern Universities Joint Matriculation Board 28, 31
Norwood Report (1943) 26, 29, 30
Nuffield Foundation 40, 48, 60, 61, 62, 73, 105, 110, 113, 115
Nursery education 87, 112, 162

Oracy 61, 62
Organisation, schools and curriculum 8, 9, 12, 14, 16, 18, 19, 22, 32, 70–1, 74, 75, 82, 89, 91, 97, 100, 116–18, 126, 134, 135–7, 138–9, 145–6

Parents 10, 11, 17, 36, 88, 134, 140, 145, 148, 150, 153, 156, 161
Payment by results 8, 9–10, 13
Physical education 114
Plowden Report 33, 87–8, 89, 91, 92, 138, 148, 149, 150
Primary and elementary schools 8, 9, 10, 12, 14, 15, 31, 32, 40, 73, 79, 87, 88, 89, 96–8, 118, 124, 127, 132–7, 143, 145
Post-elementary education 12
Publishers 38ff
Pupil power 150–1
Pupil/teacher ratio 10, 131, 162

Reading 9, 15, 61, 89, 96
Redcliffe-Maud, Lord 58
Remedial teaching 45, 65, 66, 117
Resources 42, 99, 100, 101, 116, 117, 120, 124, 130, 137, 155, 161, 162, 163
Resources for Learning Project 40, 127, 128
Revised Code, 1862 8, 9, 10
Richardson E. 119
Richmond W.K. 89
Ridgway L. & Lawton I. 134
Rural schools 7, 86, 133

Sadler M. 57
School Boards 10, 11, 12
Sciences 17, 59, 60, 114
School Leaving Certificate 26, 27, 28
School libraries 42, 124, 125
School Library Association 42
Schools Council for Curriculum and Examinations 30, 34, 35, 42, 44, 58–63, 65, 66, 69, 83, 103, 105, 110, 113, 156, 163
Schwab J.J. 54
Secondary Schools Examination Council 28, 29, 31
Secondary school organisation 14, 16, 18, 21, 31, 32, 33, 71, 72, 73, 112, 114, 116–18, 146, 163
Secular curriculum 6, 10, 22, 54
Select Committee on HMI 45
Severely subnormal pupils 112
Sixth Form chapter 3 passim; 71
Sixth Form Surveys 42
Skeffington Report (1969) 148
Snape P. 96
Specialisation of subjects 15, 16, 18, 34

INDEX

Spens Report (1938) 26, 28
Systems analysis 91

Tavistock Institute 119
Taylor L.C. 127, 128, 155
Taylor P.H. 90, 100
Taylor W. 154
Teacher education, initial training 6, 14, 108, 109, 116, 163
Teachers' Centres 40, 41, 69, 72–4, chapter 7 passim; 123
Teaching accommodation 116, 117, 120, 123, 124–6, 131, 136, 137, 145, 162
Team teaching 137–40, 141, 157
Technical subjects 61, 83
Television and teachers 110, 120, 129, 130
Textbooks 38, 39–41, 130
Timetable 18, 89, 116, 117, 137–8, 140

Townsend H.E.R. 115
Treasury Minutes, 1833–5 7
Trump J.L. 138, 139, 140

UNESCO, World Survey of Education, 1961 32
USA 6, 12, 66, 70, 85, 121, 124, 137, 145, 151
USSR 6, 48, 57

Valentine C.W. 31, 32
Vocational studies 14, 15, 16, 26, 37, 43

Wardens of Teachers' Centres 72–4, 75, 76, 101, 106
White Paper, *Education, A Framework for Expansion, 1972* 103, 108–9, 116, 128, 163–4
White W.M. 117
Wilson, Sir Percy 47